Reading & Writing 1
TARGETS
Student's Book

Virginia Evans - Jenny Dooley

Express Publishing

Published by Express Publishing

Liberty House, New Greenham Park, Newbury,
Berkshire RG19 6HW
Tel.: (0044) 1635 817 363
Fax: (0044) 1635 817 463
e-mail: inquiries@expresspublishing.co.uk
INTERNET http: //www.expresspublishing.co.uk

First published 1998
New edition 2000

ISBN   1-903128-82-X

Acknowledgements

Authors' Acknowledgements

We would like to thank all the staff at Express Publishing who have contributed their skills to producing this book. Thanks are due in particular to the following for their support and patience: Mary Palmer (editor in chief); Steve Ladd (senior editor); Ann Doyle and Sheila Howard (editorial assistants); Philippa Porter (senior production controller); E. Mavragani (art director), Debbie Costeas and Van Gard (assistant designers) and our design team; Tasso Sinerli (artist); and Debbie Ellis, Douglas Stephens, Janet Phillips, Mary Lewis, Elaine Emery, Helen Brown, Tasso Dirlis and M. Rowell. We would also like to thank those institutions and teachers who piloted the manuscript, and whose comments and feedback were invaluable in the production of the book.

Photograph Acknowledgements

Home Video Hellas for photographs on pages: 8 (bottom right © 1988 Universal City Studios Inc. All rights reserved), 42 (Romeo and Juliet), 43 (bottom right © 1988 Universal City Studios Inc. All rights reserved)

INKE for photographs on pages: 8 (middle left © INKE); picture d (© INKE), 28 (middle picture © INKE), (top right © INKE/©Mitch Gerber Corbis).

Audio Visual for photographs on pages: 8 (picture b), 33 (top right WARNER BROS © 1988 WARNER BROS INC.), 40 Mad Max, Poltergeist (MGM/UA Entertainment Co.), Star Wars (© LUCAS FILM LTD. All rights reserved), Snow White, Home Alone (© 20th Century Fox Film Corporation. All rights reserved), Gone with the Wind, 101 DALMATIANS (Walt Disney Pictures), 41 (bottom right (CBS/FOX), 42 Pocahontas (© Disney), 60 (picture d Star Wars © LUCAS FILM LTD. All rights reserved)

While every effort has been made to trace all the copyright holders, if any have been inadvertently overlooked the publishers will be pleased to make the necessary arrangements at the first opportunity.

Contents

Family Ties

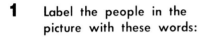

1 Label the people in the picture with these words:

mother, father, sister, brother

2 How many people are there in your family? What are their names?

3 This is Carl's project on his family. Read it and mark the statements that follow as **T** (true) or **F** (false).

I am Carl and I am nine years old. I am short and plump. I have got short brown hair and brown eyes.

This is my mother. Her name is Susan. She is thirty-four years old and she is a doctor. She has got long fair hair and blue eyes.

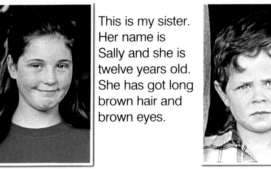

This is my father. His name is Mike. He is thirty-five years old and he is a teacher. He is tall and well-built. He has got short brown hair and big blue eyes.

This is my sister. Her name is Sally and she is twelve years old. She has got long brown hair and brown eyes.

This is my brother. His name is Tommy. He is five years old. He has got short brown hair and blue eyes.

1 Carl is nineteen years old. | F | 5 Carl's father is tall. | ☐
2 Carl is short and plump. | ☐ | 6 Carl's father has got big brown eyes. | ☐
3 Carl's mother is thirty-four years old. | ☐ | 7 Sally has got short fair hair. | ☐
4 Carl's mother is a teacher. | ☐ | 8 Tommy has got blue eyes. | ☐

4

4   Match the adjectives to their opposites.

1   tall boy   **a**   slim boy
2   plump boy   **b**   short boy
3   big eyes   **c**   long hair
4   short hair   **d**   small eyes

5   **a)** Use the words in the list to fill in the gaps below. Use one of the words twice.

mother, uncle, brother, grandfather, wife, daughter, sister, cousin, granddaughter, father, husband, aunt, son, grandmother, grandson

male ♂		female ♀	
uncle	....	*mother*	....
....	....	....	....
....	....	....	....
....	....	....	....

b) Use the words above to make pairs, as in the example.

e.g. mother - father

6   Fill in the missing forms of the verb to be.

Affirmative	Negative	Interrogative
I am	I'm not	.... I?
you	you aren't	Are you?
he	he	he?
she } is	she }	Is { she?
it	it	it?
we	we	we?
you }	you }	.... { you?
they	they	they?

7   Match the numbers to the words.

one	→ 12	twenty-three	23
twelve	29	nineteen	44
thirty-six	1	twenty-five	58
ten	36	forty-four	19
twenty-nine	10	fifty-eight	25

8   Label the pictures with the jobs in the list. Then, use the prompts to make sentences, as in the example.

gardener, nurse, reporter, porter, chef, policewoman

1   Fred / 58
    job - *gardener*
    This is Fred.
    He is fifty-eight
    years old. He
    is a gardener.

2   Kate / 29
    job - ....
    ....
    ....
    ....
    ....

3   Roy / 23
    job - ....
    ....
    ....
    ....
    ....

4   Jack / 36
    job - ....
    ....
    ....
    ....
    ....

5   Carlos / 44
    job - ....
    ....
    ....
    ....
    ....

6   Sarah / 25
    job - ....
    ....
    ....
    ....
    ....

9   Fill in the missing forms of the verb have got.

Affirmative	Negative	Interrogative
I've got	I haven't got	Have I got?
you	you	.... you ....?
he	he	he
she }	she } hasn't got	.... she ....?
it	it	it
we	we	we
you } 've got	you }	you ....?
they	they	they

10 Match the personal pronouns to the correct possessive adjectives, as in the example.

PERSONAL PRONOUNS	POSSESSIVE ADJECTIVES
I	her
you	our
he	their
she	your
it	my
we	its
you	his
they	your

11 Underline the correct words.

1 I / **My** am ten years old.
2 **She** / Her is my mother.
3 This is **we** / **our** father.
4 She is **their** / **they** sister.

12 Put these adjectives into the correct box(es). You can use some adjectives more than once.

tall, black, green, slim, short, plump, big, long, red, small, brown, blue, grey, fair, well-built

HEIGHT	*tall,*
BUILD	
HAIR	
EYES	

13 a) Read the statements under the pictures and mark them as **T** (true) or **F** (false). Then, use words from Ex. 12 to correct the false statements, as in the example.

1 Carol has got long brown hair. .. **F**..
Carol hasn't got long brown hair. She has got short red hair.

2 Lisa has got long black hair and brown eyes.
....
....
....

3 Mark is short and plump. ....
....
....
....

4 Don is slim and has got fair hair. ....
....
....
....

b) Describe your friend.

14 Use the words in the list to make sentences, as in the example.

mother, father, sister, brother, grandfather, grandmother, uncle, aunt, cousin, husband, wife, son, daughter, grandson, granddaughter

BOBBY'S FAMILY TREE

Sue & George | Harold & Rachel | Karen & Tom

David | Bobby | Mary | Ian

*e.g. This is Bobby. Karen is his **mother**. Tom is his **father**.*

15 Look at the family tree in Ex. 14 again and underline the correct words.

1 Rachel is Karen's **aunt / mother**.
2 Mary is David's **cousin / sister**.
3 Ian is Mary's **brother / husband**.
4 Harold is Bobby's **uncle / grandfather.**
5 Mary is Karen's **daughter / granddaughter.**
6 Karen is George's **wife / sister**.
7 George is Bobby's **cousin / uncle**.
8 David is Harold's **son / grandson**.

STUDY TIP

We use the possessive case **'s**:

• to show that something belongs to somebody.
  e.g. The white car is Susan's.

• to show how two or more people are related.
  e.g. Tim is Joe's brother. (= Tim and Joe are brothers.)

Note: *She's short and slim.* ('s = is)
  She's got brown eyes. ('s = has)

16 Read the sentences below and say if the 's is *possessive*, *is* or *has*.

1 John**'s** tall.
2 Laura is Tim**'s** sister.
3 Mary**'s** short and slim.
4 Peter**'s** got fair hair.
5 Steven is Mike**'s** father.
6 Tina**'s** got green eyes.

STUDY TIP

• We use a **capital letter**:
  a) when we begin a sentence.
    *e.g. **M**y father is a mechanic.*
  b) when we write the names of people.
    e.g. My mother's name is Judy.
  The personal pronoun **I** is always a capital letter.
• We put a **full stop** (.) at the end of a sentence.
    e.g. He has got green eyes.
• We can join two affirmative sentences with **and**. We can't begin a sentence with **and**.
    e.g. John is thirty years old. He is a teacher.
    *John is thirty years old **and** he is a teacher.*

17 Rewrite the following paragraph, putting full stops, capital letters and apostrophes (') where necessary.

i am henry i am thirty-five years old and i am a gardener i am tall and plump i have got short fair hair and green eyes my wifes name is martha she is thirty years old and she is a chef our daughters name is jessica and she is seven years old

WRITING

TIP

When we do a class project on our family, we write their **names**, **ages** and **jobs**. Then, we write about their **height**, **build**, **hair** and **eyes**.

18 a) Put the words into the correct order.

My / Emma / name / is... .
I / old / thirty-four / am / years ....
I / a / am / nurse ....
I / long / brown / eyes / and / have got / hair / green
....

Relation:	husband	daughter	son
Name:	James	Vicky	Phil
Age:	35	11	8
Job:	reporter	–	–
Features:	tall, short brown hair, brown eyes	long brown hair, brown eyes	very short fair hair, green eyes

b) Use the information in the table above to complete Emma's project on her family. Start like this:
This is my husband, James. He is ...

19 Look at Ex. 3 again, then do a class project on your family. Use photographs of your family to decorate your project.

Celebrities

Helena Christensen

Emma Bunton

a ....

b ....

Nicolas Cage

c ....

Tara Lipinski

d ....

Steven Spielberg

e ....

1 Label these pictures of famous people with the jobs in the list.
actor, ice-skater, film director, model, singer

2 Read the magazine article, then read the sentences below and underline the correct words.

YOUNG AND SUCCESSFUL

Tara Kristen Lipinski is a famous American ice-skater. Tara was born in 1982 and she is an Olympic gold medal winner.

Her father's name is Jack and her mother's name is Patricia. Tara hasn't got any brothers or sisters. She is an only child.

Tara is short and slim. She has got long fair hair and big blue eyes. She is a kind and hardworking person.

Tara can cook very well. She can also swim and play tennis, but she can't play basketball. Her favourite colour is purple and her favourite actor is Tom Cruise.

1 Tara is a famous **Italian** / **American** ice-skater.
2 Her **father's** / **brother's** name is Jack.
3 She has got long **brown** / **fair** hair.
4 Tara is a **hardworking** / **lazy** person.
5 She can swim and play **tennis** / **basketball**.
6 Her favourite colour is **purple** / **blue**.

UNIT 2

We use the verb **to be** to talk about somebody's:
- **job**   e.g. He **is** an actor.
- **nationality** e.g. They **are** Greek.
- **appearance**   e.g. I **am** tall and slim.
- **character**   e.g. Susan **is** a very kind person.

3   a) Match the countries to the nationalities.

1	France (Fr)	**a**	Spanish
2	Turkey (T)	**b**	English
3	Spain (Sp)	**c**	Greek
4	Poland (P)	**d**	French
5	England (Eng)	**e**	Polish
6	Italy (It)	**f**	Finnish
7	Greece (Gr)	**g**	Italian
8	Finland (Fi)	**h**	Turkish

b) Look at the information below, then ask and answer questions, as in the example.

Marie	(Fr)	1	Marie / Finnish?
Carlos	(Sp)	2	Carlos / Spanish?
Edward	(Eng)	3	Edward / Turkish?
Anouska	(Fi)	4	Anouska / French?
Renata	(P)	5	Renata / Greek?
Eleni	(Gr)	6	Eleni / English?
Gabriella	(It)	7	Gabriella / Italian?
Hassan	(T)	8	Hassan / Polish?

e.g. SA: Is Marie Finnish?
      SB: No, she isn't. She's French. Is Carlos Spanish?
      SA: Yes, he is.

STUDY TIP

We use **have/has got**:
- to show **possession**.   e.g. I've got a car.
- to talk about our **family**. e.g. I **have got** two sisters.
- to describe **physical features**.   e.g. He **has got** blue eyes.

4   a) Fill in the correct colour from the list for each balloon, as in the example.

black, green, purple, red, white, pink, orange, brown, yellow, blue

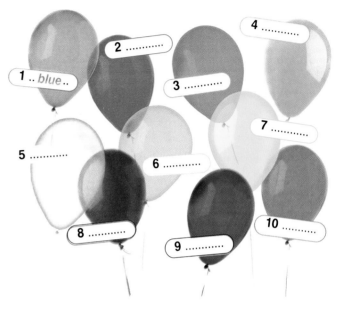

b) What is your favourite colour?

e.g. My favourite colour is yellow.

5   Look at the two people in the pictures and complete the descriptions below.

TOM   ANNE

Tom is tall and plump. He has got .... hair and brown .... He has also got a beard and ....

Anne is tall and slim. She .... hair and green ....

6   Look at the pictures on p. 8. Choose one of the celebrities and describe him/her.

9

Celebrities

STUDY TIP

- The verb **can** expresses ability. It is the same in all persons. *e.g. I can swim. He can swim.*
- **Can** always takes a **bare infinitive**. *e.g. She can read English.*

7 Match the activities (a-h) to the pictures (1-8), then say three things you can do and three things you can't do.

a	play tennis	d	cook	g swim
b	sing	e	ride a bicycle	h paint
c	dance	f	windsurf	

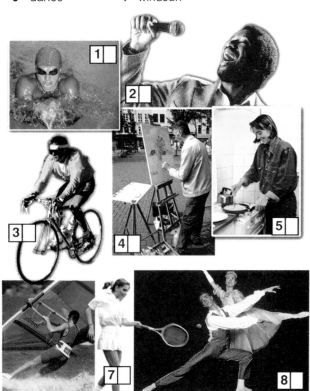

STUDY TIP

- We use **and** to join similar ideas. *e.g. He can sing **and** dance.*
- We use **but** to join contrasting ideas. *e.g. He can play tennis **but** he can't play football.*

8 Use the prompts to make sentences, as in the examples.

1 John / swim ☑ / cook ☒
John can swim but he can't cook.
2 Sarah / sing ☑ / dance ☑
Sarah can sing and dance.

3 Emily / ride a bicycle ☒ / paint ☑
....
4 Thomas / windsurf ☑ / play tennis ☑
....
5 Anna / paint ☑ / cook ☑
....
6 Chris / sing ☑ / ride a bicycle ☒
....

9 a) Look at the pictures and use words from the list to fill in the gaps.

guitarist, photographer, mechanics, pilot, clowns, artist

A I am a ....
B Tom and Ted are ....
C Jill is an ....
D Steve and I are ....
E Jack is a ....
F Charlie is a ....

b) Match the following sentences to the pictures, then say what the people can do.

1 They can make people laugh. .... *B* ....
2 She can paint beautiful pictures. ....
3 He can play the guitar very well. ....
4 We can fix cars. ....
5 He can take good photographs. ....
6 I can fly planes. ....

e.g. Clowns can make people laugh.

10   **Read the text and do the crossword.**

Jimmy Moss is twelve years old and he is a shy boy. His father, Donald Moss, is a hardworking pilot. Jimmy's mother, Shirley, is a writer and she is very clever. Jimmy has got one sister and one brother. His sister, Jill, is kind. His brother, Peter, is friendly but he is also lazy.

Across

3   Peter is a nice person. He has got a lot of friends. Peter's ... .

5   Shirley can learn fast. She's ... .

6   Jill is nice to other people. She's ... .

Down

1   Donald works very hard. He's ... .

2   Jimmy is quiet and nervous when he is with others. He's ... .

4   Peter doesn't like to work. He's ... .

11   **Read the text in Ex. 10 again and underline the adjectives which describe personality. Use these adjectives to describe the members of your family.**   *e.g. My father is clever.*

12   **Put the words into the correct order.**

1   John / but / can dance / can't sing / he

....

2   Liz / long / hair / and / eyes / brown / has got / blue

....

3   My / singer / Sting / favourite / is

....

WRITING

TIP

When we write an article about a person, we **start** by writing the person's **name**, **nationality**, **job** and **year of birth**. In the **second** paragraph we write about **his/her family**. In the **third** paragraph we **describe him/her**. We **end** our article by writing about the person's **abilities**, **favourite actor/actress/singer/colour**, etc.

13   a) **Read the following article and fill in the gaps with words from the list below.**

blue, father's, slim, singer, favourite, fair, mother's, friendly, brother, dance

▶ Emma Bunton is a famous English **1)** .... She was born in 1976 and she is one of the Spice Girls.

▶ Her **2)** .... name is Trevor and her **3)** .... name is Pauline. Emma has got a **4)** .... His name is PJ.

▶ Emma is short and **5)** .... She has got **6)** .... eyes and long **7)** .... hair. She is a **8)** .... person.

▶ Emma can **9)** .... but she can't ice-skate. Her **10)** .... singer is Madonna and her favourite colours are pink and white.

b) **Answer the following questions.**

1   Which paragraph tells us Emma's name, nationality, job and year of birth?

2   Which paragraph is about what Emma can/can't do and her favourite singer and colours?

3   Which paragraph is about Emma's appearance and character?

4   Which paragraph is about Emma's family?

14   **Use the information and the plan below to write a magazine article about Nicolas Cage. Use the picture from the Photo File section to decorate your project. Write your article in four paragraphs (60 - 80 words).**

Plan

Paragraph 1:
- Name: Nicolas Cage
- Nationality: American
- Job: actor
- Year of Birth: 1964

Paragraph 2:
- Family: father (August), mother (Joy), two brothers (Marc & Christopher)

Paragraph 3:
- Appearance: tall, slim, short brown hair, green eyes
- Character: kind, hardworking

Paragraph 4:
- Can: paint
- Can't: play football
- Favourite singer: Elvis Presley
- Favourite colour: purple

UNIT

Join the Club!

1 Which picture shows:

1	horse riding?	.....	5	hiking?	.....
2	a snooker table?	.....	6	canoeing?	.....
3	a tennis court?	.....	7	mountain biking?	.....
4	a basketball court?	.....	8	water-skiing?	.....

2 Read the advertisement for a summer camp, then read the statements and mark them as **T** (true) or **F** (false).

Looking for a suitable summer camp to send your children to in the summer holidays? Why don't you try **Sunrise Summer Camp**?

An hour's drive from London can bring you to some of England's most beautiful countryside — and Sunrise Summer Camp. All of the staff are experienced, energetic and, above all, enthusiastic. There are many activities to keep your children busy and happy all day. Behind the main building there is a games room with snooker, table tennis and many other games. There are also two basketball courts and a tennis court. Children can also go horse riding and hiking. For real adventure lovers, we have got water-skiing, canoeing and mountain biking. There is something for everyone — with lots of surprises along the way!

For more information, call 8883414 NOW!!

1 The summer camp is an hour's walk from London. ☐

2 The staff are experienced. ☐

3 There are many activities for children at the camp. ☐

4 The games room is in front of the main building. ☐

5 There are three basketball courts at the camp. ☐

6 There is canoeing for real adventure lovers. ☐

3 Match the adjectives (1-5) to their opposites (**A-E**), then read the text in **Ex. 2** and underline them. Which nouns do they describe?

1 happy   A inexperienced
2 experienced   B uninterested
3 enthusiastic   C sad
4 energetic   D ugly
5 beautiful   E lazy

4 Look at the pictures and match the pieces of equipment to the sports.

swimming   ....6....   canoeing   ....
cycling   .... skiing   ....
table tennis .... cricket   ....
golf   .... ten-pin bowling ....
basketball   .... darts   ....

1 golf clubs   2 basketball

3 bicycle   4 canoe

5 table tennis bats   6 swimming costume

7 bowling pins   8 cricket bat

9 skis   10 darts

5 Use the words in **Ex. 4** to say which sports we talk about using **play** and which using **go**.

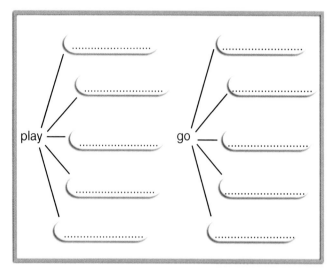

play   go

6 Use information from **Exs. 4** and **5** to make sentences, as in the example.

*e.g. To **go swimming** you need a **swimming costume**.*

7 Match the locations to the sports, then make sentences, as in the example.

*e.g. You can **play basketball on a basketball court**.*

1 on / basketball court   A golf
2 on / tennis court   B ten-pin bowling
3 in / swimming pool   C swimming
4 on / golf course   D basketball
5 on / cricket pitch   E football
6 on / football pitch   F tennis
7 at / bowling alley   G cricket

8 Fill in the gaps with words from the list.

summer, hour's, main, keep, games, basketball, adventure, beautiful

1 an .... drive
2 a .... room
3 .... lovers
4 the .... building
5 .... countryside
6 a .... court
7 to .... your children busy
8 .... holidays

13

Join the Club!

	SINGULAR	PLURAL
Affirmative	there is ...	there are ...
Negative	there isn't ...	there aren't ...
Interrogative	Is there ...?	Are there ...?
Short answers	Yes, there is. No, there isn't.	Yes, there are. No, there aren't.

- We use **there is** in the singular.
  e.g. **There is** a tennis court at the club.
- We use **there are** in the plural.
  e.g. **There are** two sports centres in our town.
  Remember: Most regular nouns form their plural by adding **-s**.   e.g. club - club**s**

9 Fill in the gaps with There is or There are, as in the example.

1 *There is* a swimming pool at the club.
2 .... two table tennis bats on the table.
3 .... a cricket pitch at the school.
4 .... some golf clubs in my car.
5 .... a games room behind the building.
6 .... a bicycle in the garage.
7 .... a tennis court at the club.
8 .... four bowling alleys at the centre.
9 .... a football pitch behind my house.
10 .... three canoes on the river.

Prepositions of Place

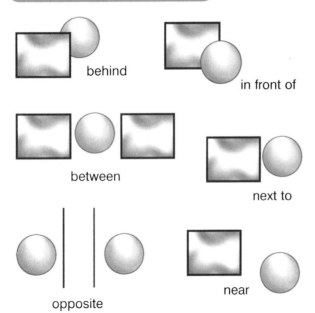

10 Look at the map of the Super Sports Centre, then read the sentences and mark them as T (true) or F (false). Finally, correct the false sentences.

1 There is a basketball court next to the football pitch.
2 There is a football pitch in front of the tennis courts.
3 There is a bowling alley behind the swimming pool and the tennis courts.
4 There is a basketball court between the cafeteria and the football pitch.
5 The Super Sports Centre is next to the bus station.

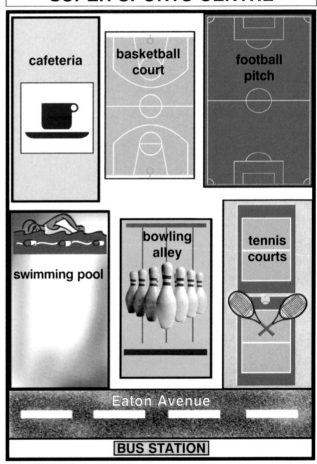

SUPER SPORTS CENTRE

cafeteria · basketball court · football pitch · swimming pool · bowling alley · tennis courts · Eaton Avenue · BUS STATION

11 Use the prepositions of place below to ask and answer questions, as in the example.

behind, in front of, next to, opposite, between

e.g. *SA: Is there a cafeteria at the Super Sports Centre?*
     SB: Yes, there is.
     SA: Where is it?
     *SB: It's **next to** the basketball court.*

STUDY TIP

- We use **commas** in lists of words.
  e.g. ... water-skiing, canoeing and mountain biking.
- We use **commas** for pauses in sentences.
  e.g. ... energetic and, above all, enthusiastic.
- We use **question marks** at the end of questions.
  e.g. Why don't you try Sunrise Summer Camp?

12 Read the text in Ex. 2 and find two question marks and seven commas.

13 Fill in the missing commas, question marks and full stops.

1 Is there a swimming pool at the club
2 There is a games room There is also a café
3 You can play football tennis and cricket there
4 Can we go canoeing at the camp
5 There are two swimming pools and a bowling alley but there isn't a tennis court
6 Your children can do many activities there such as canoeing water-skiing and mountain biking
7 The staff are friendly and experienced
8 Has the centre got a basketball court

14 Join the sentences using and or but, as in the example.

1 There is a bowling alley. There are two basketball courts.
There is a bowling alley and two basketball courts.
2 You can play snooker. You can play table tennis.
....
3 There are two swimming pools. There aren't any tennis courts. ....
4 You can't play football. You can go swimming.
....
5 The centre has got a café. The centre has got a games room. ....

WRITING

TIP

When we write an advertisement for a place, we start by mentioning the **name** of the place and **where** it is. Then, we give information about its **staff** and **facilities** and **what we can do** there. We end our advertisement by giving a **telephone number** people can call for more information. We use **adjectives** (fantastic, excellent, huge, etc) and **prepositions of place** (between, next to, etc) to make our advertisement interesting.

15 Look at the information below about the Mega Sports Centre, then use the plan and the pictures in the Photo File section to complete the advertisement for the centre. (50 - 60 words)

NOW OPEN!

MEGA SPORTS CENTRE

The best sports centre in town.

opposite the Grand Hotel on King Street

- friendly, experienced staff
- ten-pin bowling
- 2 basketball courts
- games room (5 snooker tables, 3 table tennis tables, dartboard)
- 2 swimming pools
- the Mega Café

For more information, you can call us on 8825442.

Plan

Paragraph 1: The Mega Sports Centre is the best sports centre in town. It's now open and, believe us, it's got something for everyone!

Paragraph 2: where the place is, facilities, what you can do there

Paragraph 3: For more information, you can call us on 8825442.

UNIT 4

Seasons Change

A   B

1 Match the pictures to the seasons.

spring ☐ *summer* ☐ *autumn* ☐ *winter* ☐

2 Which seasons do each of the following sentences describe?

1 It is very cold and it often snows. ....

2 It is usually hot and sunny and we often go to the beach. ....

3 It often rains, the leaves fall from the trees and we start school. ....

4 It is often warm and sunny, but sometimes it rains. There are lots of flowers.

....

C

D

3 Read Susan´s article from an international teenager magazine about her favourite season, then read the sentences and mark them as **T** (true) or **F** (false).

> ## Spring is Here!
>
> ▶1 Spring is a wonderful season. It is my favourite season because everything is so beautiful and colourful.
>
> ▶2 The weather is usually warm and sunny in spring. Beautiful flowers grow everywhere and the birds build their nests in the trees. However, the weather changes quickly. Sometimes, grey clouds appear in the sky and it rains, but after the rain, the sky turns blue again.
>
> ▶3 In spring, I spend a lot of time outdoors. I often ride my bicycle and play with my friends in the park. The countryside is lovely in spring, so my family and I often go on picnics on Sundays.
>
> ▶4 I love spring. It makes me feel happy and energetic.

1 Winter is a wonderful season. ☐
2 The weather is usually cold and rainy. ☐
3 Beautiful flowers grow everywhere. ☐
4 Susan often rides her bicycle and plays in the park. ☐
5 Spring makes Susan feel sad and lazy. ☐

4 Which paragraph:

a is about the weather and what happens in spring?

b is about Susan's feelings?

c says which Susan's favourite season is?

d is about what Susan does in spring?

5 Look at the picture showing the seasons, and put the months from the list in the correct part of the picture, in the correct order.

February, June, March, August, April, September, May, January, October, December, November, July

....
....
....

WINTER   SPRING   AUTUMN   SUMMER

....
....
....

6 Match the words to their meanings.

1	wonderful	A	very nice
2	build	B	make
3	beautiful	C	lively
4	lovely	D	amazing
5	energetic	E	birds' home
6	nest	F	very pretty

7 Fill in the gaps with words from the list.

feel, turns, build, spend, picnics, ride

1 to .... nests   4 to .... happy
2 the sky ....blue   5 to go on ....
3 to .... a bicycle   6 to .... time

8 a) In which seasons do we do these activities? Write S (for summer), A (for autumn), W (for winter) or SP (for spring).

1 make a sandcastle ☐   2 school starts ☐

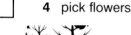

3 go skiing ☐   4 pick flowers ☐

5 go on holiday ☐   6 collect the leaves from the garden ☐

7 make a snowman ☐   8 go on picnics ☐

b) Think of some other things we do during each season and write them in the table.

WINTER

SPRING

SUMMER

AUTUMN

c) Use the prompts above and your own ideas to write two sentences about what you do during each season, as in the example.

*e.g. In the winter, I **go skiing** with my family.*

Seasons Change

9 Complete the table, as in the examples.

the morning, noon, Wednesday, August, midnight, May, the summer, the weekend, the evening, Saturday, July, Tuesday, 10 o'clock, the autumn, the afternoon

IN	*the morning,*
AT	*noon,*
ON	*Wednesday,*

10 Look at the pictures, then use the adjectives from the list to complete the sentences, as in the example.

warm, cold, rainy, windy, sunny, hot, cool

1 It snows in the winter. It's ... ***cold*** ... .

2 In the spring, there are a lot of flowers. The weather is not very hot. It's w...... .

3 In the autumn, the leaves fall from the trees. The weather isn't cold. It's c ....

4 The sun shines a lot in the summer. It's h .... and s........................... .

5 In the autumn, there are often dark clouds in the sky and it rains. Sometimes the wind blows hard. It's cloudy, r............. and w................ .

STUDY TIP

Adverbs of frequency (**never, always, sometimes, often, usually**, etc) go **before main verbs**
   e.g. I **usually go** on picnics with my family.
but **after auxiliary verbs** and the verb **to be**.
   e.g. You **can often** go skiing in winter.
   It **is usually** hot in summer.

11 Look at the chart below and use adverbs of frequency to rewrite the following sentences about yourself.

e.g. I go swimming in the summer.
*I **always** go swimming in the summer.*

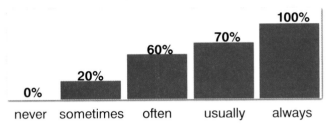

| never | sometimes | often | usually | always |
| 0% | 20% | 60% | 70% | 100% |

1 I feel happy in the spring.
2 My family and I go on holiday in the summer.
3 I go skiing in the summer.
4 We visit our grandparents at the weekend.
5 I go on picnics in the winter.

12 Look at the drawings and fill in the gaps, as in the example.

In winter, it is 1) ...cold... and 2) .... It often 3) .... and it sometimes 4) ....

In summer, it is usually 5) .... and 6) .... It is never cold, but it is sometimes 7) ....

13 Read the text below and put the verbs in brackets into the present simple.

Autumn Changes

Autumn is a beautiful season. It is my favourite season because it's cool and the trees **1)** .... **(change)** colour.

In autumn, it often **2)** .... **(rain)** and the wind **3)** .... **(blow)**. Leaves **4)** .... **(fall)** from the trees and birds **5)** .... **(fly)** to warm places.

In autumn, my mother always **6)** .... **(buy)** me a new bag, because school **7)** .... **(start)** in September. My father **8)** .... **(collect)** the leaves from the garden. Sometimes I **9)** .... **(help)** him after school. At the weekends we often **10)** .... **(visit)** my grandmother.

I **11)** .... **(like)** autumn very much. It **12)** .... **(make)** me feel relaxed and happy.

WRITING

TIP

- When we write **an article about our favourite season**, we **start** by mentioning **the season** and **why it is our favourite season**.
- In the **second** paragraph, we write about **the weather** and **nature**.
- In the **third** paragraph, we say **what we do** during that season (in the morning/afternoon/evening, at the weekend).
- In the **last** paragraph, we say **how we feel**.
- We use the **present simple** because the article is about repeated **actions/events**. We also use **adjectives** to describe the weather and our feelings.

14 a) Read Paul's article from the school newspaper about his favourite season, and put the paragraphs in the correct order.

Wonderful Winter

A I .... I do lots of things in winter. I go to school in the morning. In the evening, I stay at home and watch TV or read a book next to a warm fire. When it snows, my friends and I go to the park and make a snowman. At the weekend, my family and I go skiing in the mountains.

B I .... Winter is a lovely season. It is my favourite season because everything is beautiful when it snows.

C I .... Winter is fantastic. It makes me feel happy.

D I .... The weather is very cold. It often snows and the sky is usually cloudy. Some animals sleep all winter. There are no leaves on the trees and there aren't any flowers.

b) Read the sentences below and underline the correct words.

1 In paragraph 1, Paul introduces his favourite **weather** / **season**.
2 Paragraph 2 is about the weather and **nature** / **Paul's activities**.
3 Paragraph 3 is about Paul's **family** / **activities**.
4 Paragraph 4 is about Paul's **feelings** / **weekends**.

15 Use the plan and the prompts below to write an article for your school newspaper with the title *Summer is Great!* (50-70 words). Use the text in Ex. 3 as a model.

Plan

Paragraph 1: say why summer is your favourite
  ↓   season

Paragraph 2: describe the weather and nature
  ↓

Paragraph 3: say what you do/what happens
  ↓   during this season

Paragraph 4: say how this season makes you feel

- *favourite season* — beautiful, fantastic
- *weather and nature* — hot, sun shines, sunny, aren't any clouds, trees, green leaves, birds sing, warm sea
- *activities* — go on holiday, swim, make sandcastles, go on picnics, ride my bicycle
- *feelings* — feel happy, lively, relaxed, energetic

Time Off

1 **Match the words below to the pictures.**

1 hotel ....
2 campsite ....
3 forest ....
4 square ....
5 café ....
6 lake ....
7 beach ....

2 **Read the two postcards, then read the questions and answer them.**

Dear Emily,

I'm having a wonderful time on Capri. I'm staying at a lovely hotel in the Marina Grande.

It's a gorgeous sunny day. At the moment, I'm sitting in the town's main square. The sandy beaches here are great and the food is very tasty. I love it!

I'm really enjoying myself! I think Capri is an amazing island.

Love,
Ben

Emily Hanks
3 Bronze St
Shrewsburry
England

1 Who is on Capri?
2 Where is he staying?
3 What is the weather like on Capri?
4 What is the food like on Capri?
5 Where is Kate staying?
6 What is she doing right now?
7 Does she like Jasper National Park?
8 How do the post-cards start and how do they end?

Dear Michael,

We're having a great time here in the Rocky Mountains. We're staying at a big campsite in Jasper National Park.

It's a beautiful warm morning. Right now, I'm having breakfast at the campsite café. Bill is still sleeping. The lakes in the park are amazing and the fresh fish is always delicious.

We love it here! Jasper National Park is a fantastic place.

Yours,
Kate

Michael Spell
21 Hammersmith St
London
England

3 Fill in the gaps with words from the list.

have, beaches, sunny, fresh, breakfast, tasty, morning, square

1 .... fish
2 the main ....
3 a .... day
4 to .... a great time
5 sandy ....
6 .... food
7 a warm ....
8 to have ....

STUDY TIP

- We use the **present continuous** for **temporary** actions happening **now**, i.e. at the time of speaking
  e.g. *Right now, I am having breakfast ...*
  or **around the time of speaking**
  e.g. *We are staying at a lovely hotel in the Marina Grande.*
- We use the time expressions **now, right now, at the moment** and **at present** with the present continuous.

4 a) Write full sentences, as in the example.

1 Liz / read / in the hotel room
   Liz is reading in the hotel room.
2 Mark / explore / the forest
   ....
3 Jane / make / a sandcastle now
   ....
4 She / take / photos of the castle
   ....
5 They / buy / souvenirs at the moment
   ....
6 My sister / sunbathe / and I / write / postcards
   ....
7 They / have / coffee at a café
   ....

b) Which of the sentences in Ex. 4a describe the pictures below?

5 Look at the pictures. Then, put the verbs in the list into the present continuous and make sentences, as in the example.

ski, swim, buy souvenirs, ice-skate, sunbathe, windsurf, have lunch, read a book, play volleyball, eat watermelon

e.g. 1. She is skiing.

6 Fill in the gaps with words from the list.

herself, yourself, themselves, itself, yourselves

I'm enjoying	myself.	It's enjoying	....
You're enjoying	....	We're enjoying	ourselves.
He's enjoying	himself.	You're enjoying	....
She's enjoying	....	They're enjoying	....

21

Time Off

- We do not normally use the verbs **love**, **hate**, **like**, **dislike**, **think** and **believe** in the present continuous.
  - e.g. I **think** Capri is an amazing island.
  - **Not:** ~~I am thinking~~ Capri is an amazing island.

7 Look at the postcard extracts below and put the verbs in brackets into the present simple or present continuous.

Dear John,

I .... (have) a great time in Mexico. I .... (stay) at a lovely hotel in ...

... Mary .... (swim) in the sea and Bob .... (visit) the museum ...

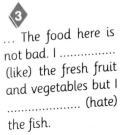

... The food here is not bad. I .... (like) the fresh fruit and vegetables but I .... (hate) the fish.

We .... (enjoy) ourselves. I .... (think) Ireland is a beautiful country.

Love,
Karen

... It .... (be) very hot today. At the moment, I .... (sunbathe). The children .... (make) a sandcastle ...

Tony .... (windsurf) now. He .... (go) windsurfing every day. We .... (have) lots of fun here.

8 Put the verbs in brackets into the present continuous. Then, match the sentences to the pictures.

1 Tony and Sue .... **(have)** a picnic at the moment.
2 John .... **(fish)** now.
3 They .... **(sail)** their boat.
4 She .... **(visit)** the ruins.
5 They .... **(eat)** ice cream.
6 She .... **(throw)** snowballs.
7 They .... **(have)** fun at the funfair.

A ☐   B ☐

C ☐   D ☐

E ☐

G ☐

F ☐

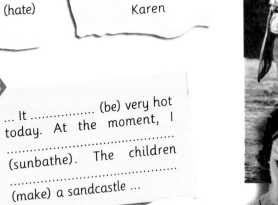

9 a) **Read these postcard extracts and answer the questions below.**

1 Who likes the place where they are?
2 Who doesn't like the place where they are?

> **A** ... I really like it here! The island is **gorgeous**.
> Love,
> Amy

> **B** ... We hate the campsite! It's a **terrible** place!
> Love,
> Peggy

> **C** ... We all love the mountains. They are **amazing**!
> Love,
> Greg

> **D** ... I really don't like the hotel I am staying at! It is **awful**!
> Yours,
> Ross

b) **Replace the adjectives in bold with words from the list.**

horrible, beautiful, wonderful, disgusting

10 **Write the postcard below in full sentences. Then, answer the questions.**

Dear Joe,
1 ▶ I / have / wonderful time / in Malta. We / stay / at a lovely

hotel in Valletta. ....
2 ▶ It /be/ warm and sunny today. Right now, I / sunbathe /

on the beach and / write / this postcard. Jill / visit / a museum

and Diane / have breakfast / at a café. The water here / be /

very blue and the beach / be / beautiful. ....
3 ▶ We / really enjoy / ourselves! I / think / Malta / be/ a

fantastic island. ....
                          Love,
                          Laura

1 Who is the postcard from?
2 Who is the postcard to?
3 How does the postcard start? How does it end?
4 Which paragraph is about the weather and what everyone is doing?
5 Which paragraph is about Laura's impressions of the place?

WRITING

TIP

- When we write **a holiday postcard to a friend**, we **start** by writing **the name of the place where we are** and **where we are staying**.
- In the **second paragraph** we write about **the weather** and **what we** (and the people we are with) **are doing at the moment**. Then, we say **what we like** about the place (*e.g. lakes, beaches, the food, etc*).
- We **finish** our postcard by giving **our impressions** of the place.
- We use the **present continuous** to write about what we are doing, and **adjectives** to make our piece of writing more interesting.

11 **Use the plan below to write a holiday postcard to a friend. (50-70 words)**

Plan

Dear ...(your friend's first name)...,

Paragraph 1: • name of the place where you are and where you are staying
⬇

Paragraph 2: • the weather
• what you (and the people you are with) are doing at the moment
⬇ • what you like about the place

Paragraph 3: • your impressions of the place
⬇

Love,
(your first name)

....

What's Cooking?

1 Look at the types of food. Which can you use to make. a) a chef's salad? b) an omelette? c) a cake? d) a sandwich?

2 Which is your favourite fruit?

3 Which of these desserts do you like?

4 Which is your favourite drink?

5 Which of these meals/snacks do we serve: a) hot? b) cold? c) both?

VEGETABLES

LETTUCE
POTATO
GREEN PEPPERS
CUCUMBERS
ONION
OLIVES
TOMATO
CARROT

FRUIT

FRUIT SALAD
APPLES
PEAR
ORANGES
STRAWBERRIES
CHERRIES
BANANA
PEACH

DESSERTS

APPLE PIE
ICE CREAM
CAKE

DRINKS

WINE
BEER
MILK
WATER
ORANGE JUICE
COKE
COFFEE

MEALS / SNACKS

OMELETTE
FISH & CHIPS
CHEF'S SALAD
BEEF & BEANS
PIZZA
CHICKEN & RICE
SANDWICH
SOUP
SAUSAGES

VARIOUS

EDAM CHEESE
MAYONNAISE
OLIVE OIL
HAM
VINEGAR
MUSTARD
TOMATO KETCHUP
BACON
FLOUR
BUTTER
SUGAR
BREAD
PEPPER
EGGS
SALT

STUDY TIP

- We form the **imperative** with the bare infinitive of the verb. We do not use a personal pronoun.
  - e.g. **Open** the door.   Not: ~~You~~ open the door.
- We use the imperative to give **instructions** and **orders**.
  - e.g. Slice the cheese. Boil the eggs.

6   Match the instructions to the pictures.

cut up the chicken, break the eggs into a bowl, peel the banana, chop the onion, beat the mixture, mix all the ingredients well, slice the meat, add the sugar, pour the coffee

1   .... *cut up the* ....
.... *chicken* ....

2   ....
....

3   ....
....

4   ....
....

5   ....
....

6   ....
....

7   ....
....

8   ....
....

9   ....
....

7   Look at these pictures showing ways of cooking, then match the words in the list to the pictures. Finally, make sentences, as in the example.

eggs, potatoes, cake, biscuits, fish, bread, rice, sausages

e.g. You can boil eggs in a saucepan.
You can fry eggs in a frying pan.

1   boil/saucepan
eggs, ...
....

2   bake/oven
....
....

3   grill/barbecue
....
....

4   fry/frying pan
eggs, ...
....

Plurals

Study these examples.

egg	➡	egg**s**
pear	➡	pear**s**
olive	➡	olive**s**
strawberry	➡	strawberr**ies**
potato	➡	potato**es**
sandwich	➡	sandwich**es**
lettuce leaf	➡	lettuce lea**ves**

8   Fill in the correct plurals.

1   cake - ....
2   cherry - ....
3   biscuit - ....
4   tomato - ....
5   peach - ....
6   loaf - ....
7   onion - ....
8   carrot - ....

What's Cooking?

- Words like **beef, bread, milk, spaghetti, water, oil, sugar, flour, butter**, etc are **uncountable**. However, we can use these nouns after words, such as **bottle, piece, slice, loaf, cup, glass, kilo/grams, carton, bowl, packet, teaspoon/tablespoon**, etc.
- **Remember:** a + consonant sound   e.g. **a banana**
  an + vowel sound   e.g. **an apple**

a **bottle** of wine

a **piece** of cheese

some **slices** of ham

a **loaf** of bread

a **cup** of coffee

a **glass** of juice

a **kilo** of meat /
1000 **grams** of meat

a **bowl** of sugar

a **tablespoon** of
flour

a **tin** of fish

a **carton** of milk

a **packet** of
spaghetti

9 Look at the prompts below and cross out the incorrect word, as in the example.

1 a cup of tea / coffee / ~~bread~~
2 two kilos of beef / beer / ham
3 a bottle of coffee / water / wine
4 a piece of ham / cheese / flour
5 a slice of bread / sugar / ham
6 a glass of milk / water / soup
7 a bowl of wine / ice cream / soup
8 a packet of spaghetti / rice / juice
9 a tablespoon of chicken / salt / olive oil

10 a) Read this recipe for a chef's salad and fill in the gaps with words from the list.

add, boil, cut, mix, pour, put, remove, serve, slice

Chef's Salad

Ingredients	Dressing
2 eggs	2 tablespoons mayonnaise
8 lettuce leaves	1 tablespoon tomato ketchup
150g Edam cheese	1 tablespoon vinegar
4 slices ham	1 tablespoon olive oil
1 small cucumber	salt and pepper
1 large tomato	

Instructions

- (1) .... the eggs for 10 minutes.
- (2) .... up the lettuce leaves and put them into a salad bowl.
- Cut the cheese and the ham into small pieces and add them to the bowl.
- (3) .... the cucumber and cut the tomato into pieces, then add them to the bowl.
- (4) .... the shell from the eggs, slice them and put them on top of the salad.

For the dressing

- (5) .... the mayonnaise, tomato ketchup, olive oil and vinegar into a small bowl and (6) .... them well.
- (7) .... salt and pepper.
- Finally, (8) .... the dressing over the salad.
- (9) .... with fresh bread.

b) Read the recipe again, then read the following statements and mark them as **T** (true) or **F** (false).

1 You need two eggs to make a chef's salad. ☐

2 Boil the eggs for 15 minutes. ☐

3 Cut the cheese and the ham into big pieces. ☐

4 Cut the tomato into pieces. ☐

5 Serve with fresh vegetables. ☐

- We use **How many ...?** with **countable** nouns.
  e.g. How many eggs are there?
- We use **How much ...?** with **uncountable** nouns.
  e.g. How much cheese do we need?

11　Fill **in** much **or** many.

A: Let's make a pizza for dinner.

B: That's a good idea!

A: Yes, but I need the ingredients. Can you go to the supermarket and get them for me?

B: Of course. How **1)** .... pizzas do you want to make?

A: Just one, so I need one frozen pizza base, tomatoes, cheese, mushrooms, green peppers and ham.

B: How **2)** .... tomatoes do you want?

A: Five, please.

B: And how **3)** .... cheese?

A: About 200 grams.

B: Okay. How **4)** .... mushrooms do you need?

A: Buy me about 50 grams, please.

B: What about green peppers? How **5)** .... do you want?

A: Just one. Oh, don't forget the ham.

B: How **6)** .... ham do you need?

A: Um, get me ten slices of ham, please.

- We use **some** in **affirmative statements** with uncountable nouns and countable nouns in the plural.
  *e.g. I need **some cheese** and **some tomatoes**.*
- We use **any** in **questions** and **negative statements** with uncountable nouns and countable nouns in the plural.
  *e.g. Is there **any butter** in the fridge?*
  *I haven't got **any peaches**.*

12　Fill **in** how much, how many, some **or** any.

A: Mum, I'm hungry.

B: Do you want a Mediterranean omelette?

A: Yes ... but I don't know how to make it.

B: Alright. Come on then − let's make one together.

A: Thanks, Mum! Okay. I need **1)** .... eggs, but **2)** .... do I need?

B: Two. You also need a small onion, a small green pepper, a large tomato and **3)** .... butter.

A: **4)** .... butter?

B: About 25 grams.

A: Do I need **5)** .... salt and pepper?

B: Yes, you do.

A: Do I need **6)** .... flour?

B: No, you don't need **7)** .... flour. Now, cut the onion, green pepper and tomato into small pieces.

A: Like this?

B: Yes, that's right. Put the butter into the frying pan.

A: Do I put the vegetables in the frying pan now?

B: Yes. Fry them for about three minutes. Okay, break the eggs into a bowl. Add **8)** .... salt and pepper. Good. Now, beat them well .... like that. Right, I think the vegetables are ready now, so add the eggs to the frying pan. There ... now cook it for three minutes.

A: Is it ready?

B: Not yet. Turn the omelette over. Have we got **9)** .... bread?

A: Yes, we have.

B: Okay! Serve it with bread, and it's delicious.

A: Is the omelette ready now?

B: Yes. Mm ... I think *I'm* hungry now. Can I try it?

A: Oh, alright then!

WRITING

TIP

- When we write a **recipe**, we **start** by giving the **name of the dish** the recipe is for. Then, we **list** all the **ingredients**. After that we write the **instructions in the correct order**. We write each step on a separate line.
- We always use the **imperative** when we write recipes.

13　Use the information from Ex. 12 and the picture from the Photo File section to write a recipe for an omelette for a cookery competition. Write your recipe using the plan below. Use Ex. 10a as a model.

Plan

- Name of the dish the recipe is for.
- Write the list of the ingredients.
- Write the instructions in the correct order.

A Day in the Life of ...

1
- Do you know who this person is?
- Why is she famous?
- What time do you think she gets up?
- What time do you think she goes to the Detroit Skating Club?
- How many hours of practice do you think she has every day? Do you think she works with a coach?
- Do you think she goes to bed early?

2 Read the article about a typical day in the life of Tara Lipinski, then read sentences 1-6 and mark them as **T** (true) or **F** (false).

A Day in the Life of Tara Lipinski

Tara Lipinski, the famous Olympic gold medallist ice-skater, tells us about a typical day in her life.

"My weekdays are quite tiring. I get up at half past seven and have breakfast. At half past eight, Mum drives me to the Detroit Skating Club. I practise from nine o'clock till lunchtime at twelve o'clock.

I usually eat a turkey sandwich and some biscuits for lunch, and I drink some fresh juice. My lunch break finishes at one o'clock, then I work with my coaches till a quarter to three. After that my mother drives me home. I start lessons at home at three o'clock.

You see, I can't go to a normal school because I have ice-skating practice in the mornings.

When my teacher leaves, at about half past six, I make dinner with my mother. We have dinner at about half past seven, then, at eight o'clock, I do my homework or watch TV. I usually have a shower at about nine o'clock, then I go to bed at about half past nine.

What do I do in my free time? Well, I go shopping, meet my friends, play tennis or go swimming. I don't have much free time, but I enjoy every minute of it."

1 "At half past seven, Mum drives me to the Detroit Running Club." ☐

2 "I usually eat a turkey sandwich and some biscuits for dinner." ☐

3 "I start lessons at school at three o'clock." ☐

4 "When my teacher leaves, at about half past six, I watch TV with my mother." ☐

5 "I don't have much free time." ☐

6 The first paragraph is about Tara's free-time activities. ☐

3 Study the table below, then look at the clock faces and write the time in both ways.

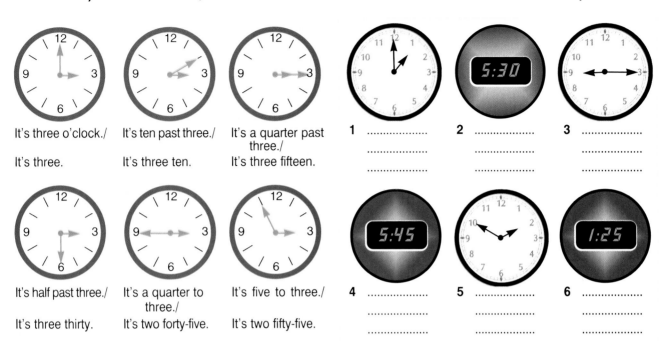

It's three o'clock./

It's three.

It's ten past three./

It's three ten.

It's a quarter past three./

It's three fifteen.

1 ....
....
....

2 ....
....
....

3 ....
....
....

It's half past three./

It's three thirty.

It's a quarter to three./

It's two forty-five.

It's five to three./

It's two fifty-five.

4 ....
....
....

5 ....
....
....

6 ....
....
....

4 Read the article about Tara again and fill in the table. Then, talk about Tara's daily routine.

7:30 *Tara gets up at seven thirty and has breakfast.*

8:30 Then, ...
....
....

9:00 - 12:00 ....
....
....

12:00 - 1:00 After that, ...
....
....

1:00 - 2:45 Then, ...
....
....

2:45 ....
....
....

3:00 - 6:30 ....
....
....

6:30 After that, ...
....
....

7:30 ....
....
....

8:00 Then, ...
....
....

9:00 After that, ...
.... , then

9:30 ....

5 Tick the activities that you do every day, and fill in the times. Then, use your notes, as well as your own ideas, to talk about your daily routine. Use first, then, after that, next.

MORNING

get up	☐	drive to work	☐ ....
have a shower	☐	catch the bus	☐ ....
get dressed	☐	start lessons	☐ ....
have breakfast	☐	start work	☐ ....
leave home	☐	have a break	☐ ....

AFTERNOON

have lunch	☐	finish work	☐ ....
finish school	☐	go home	☐ ....

EVENING

do homework	☐	watch TV	☐ ....
cook dinner	☐	listen to music	☐ ....
have dinner	☐	go out	☐ ....
have a shower	☐	play cards	☐ ....
have a bath	☐	go to bed	☐ ....

6 Look at the activities in these photographs. How often do you do each activity in your free time - never, rarely, sometimes, often, usually or always?

e.g. I never go fishing in my free time.

go fishing

watch TV

go swimming

go to the cinema

go for a walk

go on a picnic

go roller-skating

go shopping

meet my friends

read a book

play computer games

go to a disco

7 What do you do in your free time? Choose activities from Ex. 6 as well as your own ideas.

STUDY TIP

We use the **present simple** to talk about **permanent states**, **repeated actions** and **daily routines**.
*e.g. We **watch** TV in the evening.*

AFFIRMATIVE	NEGATIVE
I/You/We/They **work** ... He/She/It **works** ...	I/You/We/They **don't** work ... He/She/It **doesn't** work ...

QUESTIONS	SHORT ANSWERS
Do I/you/we/they **work**? **Does** he/she/it **work**?	Yes, I/you/we/they **do**. No, I/you/we/they **don't**. Yes, he/she/it **does**. No, he/she/it **doesn't**.

SPELLING

I work - he work**s**	I kiss - he kiss**es**
I go - he go**es**	I fish - he fish**es**
I try - he tr**ies**	I watch - he watch**es**

WRITING

TIP

- When we write about somebody's **daily routine**, we **start** by saying **who the person is** and what his/her **job** is.
- In the **second** paragraph we write what he or she does **every morning**.
- In the **third** paragraph we write what the person does **every afternoon**.
- In the **fourth** paragraph we write what the person does **every evening**.
- In the **last** paragraph we write what he or she likes doing in his or her **free time**.

We use the **present simple** to write about someone's daily routine.

8   Read the paragraphs below and: a) number them in the correct order; b) put the verbs in brackets into the present simple; c) say what each paragraph is about.

A ☐   In his free time, Tim .... **(like)** playing tennis or going for walks.

B ☐   Tim .... **(have)** a sandwich for lunch at about half past twelve, then he .... **(teach)** till three. He .... **(stay)** at school till half past three. After that he .... **(go)** home and .... **(prepare)** his lessons for the next day.

C ☐   Tim .... **(get up)** at seven o'clock every morning. He .... **(have)** a shower and then he has breakfast. Tim .... **(catch)** the bus to work at about eight. He usually .... **(arrive)** at school at a quarter to nine and .... **(start)** his lessons at nine.

D ☐   In the evening, Tim .... **(help)** his children with their homework. He .... **(have)** dinner with his wife, Julia, and the children at about half past six. After that, they watch TV or play board games. The children .... **(go)** to bed at eight o'clock, then Tim and Julia .... **(listen)** to music until bedtime, at about half past ten.

E ☐   Tim Franks is a teacher. He .... **(work)** in a primary school in London.

9   Patty Stevens works as a celebrity casting agent at The Talent Corporation in London. Read what she says and answer the questions.

1   What does Patty do in the morning?
2   What does Patty do in the afternoon?
3   What does Patty do in the evening?
4   What does Patty do in her free time?

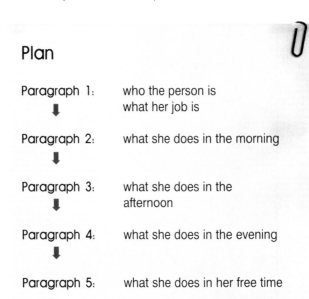

> I have breakfast at work at about 10:30 am. I also read the newspaper.

> In my free time, I meet my friends or go on a picnic.

> My day starts early. I get up at 8:30 am.

> I rarely have lunch because I'm very busy.

> I drive to work. I usually arrive there at about 10 am.

> I leave the office at about 5 pm.

> From 1 pm till 4:30, I have meetings with various celebrities.

> Sometimes I work late and I don't get home till midnight.

> I often have dinner with a celebrity at about 6:30 pm.

10   Use the information from Ex. 9 and the plan below to write a magazine article about Patty's daily routine in the Photo File section (**100-120 words**). Use Ex. 8 as a model.

Plan

Paragraph 1:	who the person is what her job is
Paragraph 2:	what she does in the morning
Paragraph 3:	what she does in the afternoon
Paragraph 4:	what she does in the evening
Paragraph 5:	what she does in her free time

What's the Story?

1 Look at the pictures. Which picture(s) show(s):

a) a military air base?
b) a soldier with a parachute?
c) tea, a cake and biscuits?
d) a broken table?
e) a plane flying over?

A

2 Read the sentences, then put them into the correct speech bubbles.

- "Watch out!"
- "I'm afraid there isn't any tea for you!"
- "Would you like some sugar?"
- "I'm so sorry! My parachute didn't open on time!"

B

3 Study the following table, then use the verbs in the past form to complete the story below.

REGULAR		IRREGULAR			
Present	Past	Present	Past	Present	Past
ask	asked	be	was/were	fall	fell
decide	decided	begin	began	have	had
land	landed	bring	brought	hear	heard
look	looked	can	could	say	said
pour	poured	come	came	sit	sat

C

An Unexpected Visitor

One sunny afternoon last May, my mother and I **1)** .... **(decide)** to have tea in the garden. We live near a small military air base and we like to watch the planes fly over. My mother **2)** .... **(bring)** out some delicious biscuits, a cake and a pot of tea. She **3)** .... **(pour)** me some tea and **4)** .... **(ask)** me, "Would you like some sugar?"

Before I **5)** .... **(can)** answer, we **6)** .... **(hear)** a loud cry: "Watch out!" Then, suddenly, a soldier **7)** .... **(land)** on the table. Mum and I **8)** .... **(fall)** off our chairs in surprise.

When I **9)** .... **(look)** up, the soldier **10)** .... **(be)** on the broken table with a parachute over his head! "I'm *so* sorry!" he **11)** .... **(say)**. "My parachute didn't open on time!" Mum and I both **12)** .... **(look)** at him strangely, then we all **13)** .... **(begin)** to laugh. "I'm afraid there isn't any tea for you!" Mum **14)** .... **(say)** cheerfully.

Fortunately, we **15)** .... **(be)** all okay. The next day, the soldier **16)** .... **(come)** back with a huge box of cakes for us. We all **17)** .... **(have)** tea together, but this time we **18)** .... **(sit)** in the dining room!

D

32

STUDY TIP

- When we write a **story**, it is important to decide on the **events** and write them **in the order they happened**.
- We can use **time words** (*e.g. first, then, later, after that, next, finally, before, after, when, etc*) to link the events.

4 Read the story again, then look at the sentences below and number them in the order they happened.

- ☐ A soldier landed on the table.
- ☐ We all began to laugh.
- ☐ Mum brought out biscuits, a cake and a pot of tea.
- ☐ The soldier came back with a box of cakes.
- ☐ We fell off our chairs.
- ☐ We heard a loud cry.
- ☐ We all had tea together in the dining room.
- ☐ 1 We decided to have tea in the garden.

5 Underline the correct words / phrases.

1 My father's a pilot in the air force. He works at a **skating club / military air base**.
2 I **watch / see** TV every night.
3 Could you **put / pour** me a glass of Coke, please?
4 The police helicopter **flew / blew** over the city.
5 The soldier jumped out of the plane and opened his **parachute / umbrella**.
6 **Fortunately / Unfortunately**, I passed my driving test.
7 "It's a lovely day!" Dad said **anxiously / cheerfully**.

STUDY TIP

To start a story, we say **where** and **when** the story takes place, **who** the people in the story are, and **what happened** first.

6 Read the story in Ex. 3 again, then read the questions below and circle the correct answer.

1 Where does the story take place?
a) in the park **b)** in the garden
2 How many people are there in the story?
a) three **b)** two
3 When does the story take place?
a) one morning last May **b)** one afternoon last May

4 What was the weather like?
a) cold **b)** sunny
5 What did they decide to do?
a) have tea in the garden **b)** have dinner in the garden
6 What happened then?
a) They saw a plane. **b)** They heard a loud cry.

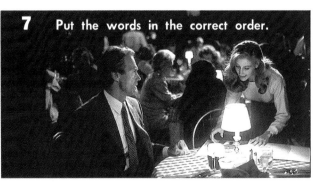

7 Put the words in the correct order.

1 Last / went / a / night / to / restaurant / I
....
2 I / an / empty / for / at / and / down / waited / table / my friend / sat
....
3 Suddenly / came / my / good-looking / a / table / woman / towards
....
4 "Who / she / is?" / wondered / I
....

8 **a)** Read the short story below, and put the verbs in brackets into the past simple.

A ☐ On my first night there, I .... **(put on)** my pyjamas and then I .... **(get)** into bed. Suddenly, I .... **(hear)** a loud noise like a fire alarm. "Oh no! A fire!" I .... **(think)**.

B ☐ The manager of the hotel .... **(laugh)** and .... **(say)**, "That wasn't a fire alarm, Mr Dodd. It was the shop alarm next door. Someone .... **(press)** it by mistake!"

C ☐ I .... **(jump)** out of bed quickly and .... **(open)** the door. There .... **(be)** no one around, so I .... **(run)** downstairs to the reception. Everyone .... **(look)** at me strangely. "Where's the fire?" I .... **(ask)** anxiously.

D ☐ Last year, I .... **(go)** to Rome on holiday. I .... **(stay)** at an expensive hotel near the city centre.

b) Put the paragraphs in the correct order and read them aloud.

9 Underline the correct words.

1 **After** / **When** I walked into the kitchen, I saw a man on the floor.
2 **First** / **Then** I poured the coffee, then I made the toast.
3 He put on his coat and shut the door. **Then** / **After**, he ran quickly down the street.
4 **When** / **Later**, she realised all the money was gone.
5 **After** / **When** that, June immediately called the police.
6 First, she checked that no one else was hurt. **Next** / **After**, she climbed carefully into the back of the ambulance.
7 **Before** / **Finally**, she put the cake in the oven to bake.
8 I had breakfast **before** / **later** I went to work.
9 **After** / **First** I drank the wine, I felt quite sleepy.

10 Use the adverbial phrases in list **A** and the actions in list **B** to make sentences, as in the example.

A
last summer
a month ago
three years ago
yesterday morning
the day before yesterday
on my seventh birthday
last Christmas
last weekend
last night

B
go camping
go on holiday
meet some friends
learn to ride a bicycle
stay at home and relax
visit my grandmother
get lots of presents
have a party
go to work

e.g. **Last summer, I went on holiday** to France.

....
....
....
....
....
....
....
....
....
....

STUDY TIP

When we **end** a story, we write **what happened in the end**. We can also write **how the people** in the story **felt**.

11 Read the story in Ex. 3 again. How does it end? How do the people feel?

12 a) How does each person feel? Choose adjectives from the list below.
proud, happy, surprised, angry, confused, tired, sad, scared

1 .... happy ....   5 ....

2 ....   6 ....

3 ....   7 ....

4 ....   8 ....

b) Read the sentences and fill in the correct adjective from the list above.

1 Luckily, Jane wasn't hurt. She was very .... to be safe and warm after such a terrible day.
2 Ann couldn't believe her eyes. She was very .... to see her husband on the six o'clock news.
3 He looked at the damage to his car and started to shout. He was very ....
4 "Who is this letter from?" she said. "I don't understand." She was very ....
5 Boris was very .... The only thing he wanted to do was to go to bed.
6 Unfortunately, Sammy's dog died. Sammy was very .... He lost a very good friend that day.
7 Little Jimmy reached the finishing line first. We were all .... of him.
8 She saw the man take something out of his pocket. It was a gun! Suddenly, she felt very ....

34

WRITING

TIP

When we write a **story**, we divide it into **four paragraphs**.

- We **start** our story by mentioning the **time**, the **place** and the **people** involved.
- In the **second** and **third** paragraphs, we describe what happened. We write the **events one after the other**, in the order they happened.
- We **end** our story by describing **what happened in the end** and **how the people felt**.
  We use the **past simple** and **time words** (first, after that, then, etc) in stories.

13   a) The following pictures show what happened to Jim when he decided to take his pet snake, Slippy, to the vet. Look at the pictures and answer the questions.

PICTURE A
1 Where is Jim?
2 What time is it?
3 Who else is with him?

PICTURE B
1 Where are Jim and Slippy?
2 Who else is with them?
3 How do the men feel?
4 What is one of the men holding?
5 What do they tell Jim to give them?

PICTURE C
1 Why are the two men running away?
2 How do they feel?

PICTURE D
1 Where are Jim and Slippy?
2 How does Jim feel?

ON THE PLATFORM

b) Fill in the speech bubbles in the pictures with the items below.
- "Help! A snake!"
- "Give me your bag, now!"

c) Look at the pictures again. Use the list of words below to help you tell the story using the past simple.

- afternoon - two weeks ago - Jim - decide - take pet snake - vet - put Slippy - sports bag - go - underground station
- on the train - notice - two large men - feel frightened - come up to him - give bag! - knife in hand - give bag
- take bag - open it - Slippy's head pop out - help! - snake! - run towards door
- train - stop - next station - jump off train - run away - feel happy - proud

14   Use the information from Ex. 13 and the plan below to write a story (80 - 100 words) for a story competition in your school magazine. The title for your story is: *A Hero For a Day!* Begin like this:

One afternoon, two weeks ago, Jim decided to take his pet snake, Slippy, to the vet. He put ...

Plan

Paragraph 1:   mention the time, place and people involved
↓

Paragraphs 2-3:   develop the story (events one after the other)
↓

Paragraph 4:   describe what happened in the end & people's feelings

AT HOME

ON THE TRAIN

UNIT 9

All Creatures Great and Small

goldfish

cat

horse

monkey

rabbit

parrot

hamster

snake

dog

1 Look at the pictures and answer the questions below.

a) Have you got a pet? What's its name?
b) Which of these animals is your favourite?
c) Which animal do you think is ...
the most expensive to keep?
the noisiest?
the most independent?
the most intelligent?
the most loyal?
the most playful?
the most dangerous?

2 a) What is a topic sentence?

A A sentence which ends a paragraph.
B A sentence which starts a paragraph and summarises what the paragraph is about.

b) **The following sentences are topic sentences. Read them, then read the article and choose from the sentences a to d the one which fits each gap (1-4).**

a However, keeping a dog in the house can be difficult.
b A pet can change your life.
c In conclusion, I believe that, despite those minor problems, dogs still make the best pets.
d Dogs are wonderful pets.

IS "MAN'S BEST FRIEND" THE BEST PET?

1 Dogs in particular, can make your life more interesting and that is why they are the most popular ones in the world.

2 Children love them because they are very playful. Also, they obey commands better than most other animals as they are very obedient. What is more, they never run away from their owners because they are very loyal pets.

3 Firstly, they need a lot of space as they are very energetic animals. Secondly, they can cause problems with your neighbours. They can be very noisy sometimes.

4 Give your dog a little love and attention and you can have a friend for life.

c) Read the article again and find the good points and the bad points about having a pet dog.

d) What is the writer's opinion about dogs? In which paragraph does he state his opinion?

3 Fill in the gaps with words from the list.

love, friend, obey, more, cause, problems

1 what is ....
2 to .... commands
3 a .... for life
4 to .... problems
5 minor ....
6 .... and attention

4 Underline the correct words in bold.

1 Rabbits are **quiet / noisy**. They don't make a lot of noise.
2 Cats are very **lazy / funny**. All they do is eat and sleep.
3 Goldfish don't eat a lot, so they are **cheap / expensive** to keep.
4 Cats are **loyal / independent**, so they don't need a lot of attention.
5 Dogs are very **playful / clever**, so you can train them to do things.
6 Be careful with snakes! They are very **dangerous / intelligent**.

5 Put the adjectives in Ex. 4 into the correct column, then choose two adjectives from each column and write your own sentences.

*e.g. Hamsters are **quiet** animals.*

Good Points	Bad Points
quiet, ...	*noisy,* ....
....	....
....	....
....	....
....	....
....	....

6 Fill in the correct adjective from the list.

obedient, noisy, cheap, quiet, dangerous, clever

1 Parrots are ...*clever*... . They can learn to talk easily.
2 Rabbits are .... animals. They don't make a lot of noise.
3 Snakes are .... They can hurt you.
4 Monkeys are .... animals. They are rarely quiet.
5 Dogs are .... They obey commands very well.
6 Goldfish are .... pets. They don't cost much money to buy and keep.

7 Complete the table, then say how we form the comparative and superlative forms of adjectives.

Adjectives	Comparatives	Superlatives
energetic	more energetic	....
....	cheaper	the cheapest
dangerous	more dangerous	....
good	better	....
....	lazier	the laziest
bad	....	the worst
expensive	more expensive	....
loyal	....	the most loyal
big	....	the biggest
....	friendlier	the friendliest
old	older	....
obedient	....	the most obedient
safe	safer	....

8 Fill in the comparative form of the verbs in brackets, as in the example.

1 A: Goldfish are ..... *more expensive* ..... **(expensive)** to keep than horses.
   B: Actually, I think they are ..... *cheaper* ..... **(cheap)**.
2 A: Cats are .... **(energetic)** than dogs.
   B: Actually, I think they are .... **(lazy)**.
3 A: Horses are .... **(quiet)** than cats.
   B: That's not true. They are .... **(noisy)**.
4 A: Snakes are .... **(safe)** than monkeys.
   B: That's not true. They are .... **(dangerous)**.
5 A: Monkeys are .... **(obedient)** than dogs.
   B: That's not true. They are .... **(naughty)**.

9 Read the first sentence, then complete the second with the correct superlative.

1 A: Dogs are obedient.
 B: I agree. I think they are the ..... *most obedient* ..... pets of all.
2 A: Cats are lazy.
 B: I agree. I think they are the .... pets of all.
3 A: Parrots are noisy.
 B: I agree. I think they are the .... pets of all.
4 A: Horses are strong.
 B: I agree. I think they are the .... pets of all.
5 A: Goldfish are boring.
 B: I agree. I think they are the .... pets of all.

STUDY TIP

- We use **firstly, secondly, also, what is more**, etc to list points.
 *e.g. Dogs are obedient. **What is more**, they are loyal.*
- We use **however, on the other hand**, etc to introduce opposing ideas.
 *e.g. Dogs are loyal. **On the other hand**, they are noisy.*

10 Read the article in Ex. 2 again. Which words/phrases does the writer use to: a) list points; b) introduce opposing ideas?

11 Underline the correct words/phrases in bold.

1 Rabbits are cute. **What is more / However**, they are dirty.
2 Monkeys are playful. **On the other hand / Also**, they are noisy.
3 Goldfish are easy to care for. **Also / However**, they are cheap to keep.
4 **Firstly / However**, dogs are loyal. Secondly, they are obedient.
5 Cats are independent. **On the other hand / Also**, they are lazy.
6 Horses need a lot of space. **What is more / However**, they are expensive to keep.
7 Hamsters are quiet. **Firstly / Also**, they are easy to care for.
8 Firstly, snakes are expensive to buy. **However / Secondly**, they are dangerous.
9 Parrots are noisy. **On the other hand / Also**, they are clever.
10 Dogs are very friendly. **What is more / However**, they are playful.

12 a) Read the article and fill in the gaps with the correct words/phrases from the list. Then, underline the topic sentences.

also, firstly, on the other hand, what is more, secondly

"Pretty Polly" — Popular Pets, Despite the Problems

Are you looking for a pet? Parrots are a very popular choice.

Parrots are great pets. **1)** .... , they are beautiful birds because they are brightly coloured. **2)** .... , parrots are entertaining and amusing. They can make you laugh with the things they say. **3)** .... , they aren't difficult to look after as they don't need any exercise.

4) .... , parrots can cause problems. They can embarrass you as they often repeat rude words from the TV or radio. **5)** .... , you can't leave them alone all day because they need to have company.

In conclusion, I think that, despite their bad points, parrots make excellent pets. It's great fun teaching them to say things, and they can be very entertaining companions.

b) List the good and bad points about parrots. What reason does the writer give for each point? Finally, use your notes to talk about parrots.

Good Points	Reasons
•	• ....
•	• ....
•	• ....
•	• ....

Bad Points

- ....
  ....
  ....
- ....
  ....
  ....

Reasons

- ....
  ....
  ....
- ....
  ....
  ....

13 Match the good and bad points about hamsters to the reasons, then write full sentences to complete the paragraphs below. Use **as** or **because** to join the points to the reasons.

Good Points

1 make great pets for children

2 not expensive to keep

3 easy to look after

Reasons

a they don't need much attention

b they are small and cute

c they don't eat a lot

Bad Points

1 aren't fun to play with

2 they can bite you

Reasons

a they are frightened of people

b you can't teach them to do tricks

Hamsters are wonderful pets. **Firstly,** *hamsters make great pets for children as they are small and cute.* **Secondly,** *they* ....
....
....

On the other hand, keeping a hamster as a pet has its bad points. They aren't fun to play with **because** ....
....
....
....

WRITING

> ## TIP
>
> When we write **an article giving the good and bad points** about keeping a particular pet, we divide it into four paragraphs.
>
> - We **start** by saying **what kind of pet** we are going to write about.
> - In the **second paragraph**, we list the **good points** with **reasons.**
> - In the **third paragraph**, we list the **bad points** with **reasons.**
> - We **end** our article by giving our **opinion.**
>
> We list points with **firstly, secondly, also, what is more,** etc. We use words and expressions such as **however, on the other hand,** etc to introduce **opposing ideas.** We can use **as** or **because** to link the good or bad points to their reasons. We express our opinion with **I think, I believe, In my opinion,** etc.

14 Use the prompts and the plan below, as well as the picture and the beginning and ending given in the Photo File section, to complete the article (80 - 100 words) with the title *Cats Can Make the Best Pets.* Use the texts in Ex. 2 and Ex. 12 as models.

Good Points & Reasons	Bad Points & Reasons
• make great companions → they are very playful	• can't teach them to do tricks → they don't obey commands
• easy to look after → they don't need much attention	• can destroy your furniture → they need to sharpen their claws
• cheap to keep → their food doesn't cost much	

Plan

Paragraph 1:   kind of pet
↓
Paragraph 2:   good points and reasons
↓
Paragraph 3:   bad points and reasons
↓
Paragraph 4:   your opinion

Mad Max 3

Poltergeist

Star Wars

Lights! Camera! ACTION!

1 a) Use the types of films in the list below to answer the questions that follow.

Snow White and the Seven Dwarfs

a romance
an action film
a comedy
a science-fiction film
a horror film
a cartoon

What type of film:
a) is full of funny scenes? ....
b) is about two people in love? ....
c) is full of action and danger? ....
d) has frightening scenes? ....
e) is about space technology, aliens or life in the future?
   ....
f) has moving drawings? ....

b) **What type is each of the films in the pictures?**

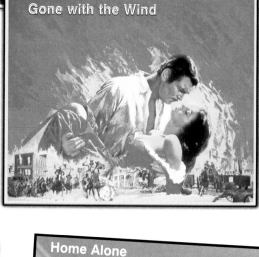

Gone with the Wind

2 Read Tom Brown's film review for his school newspaper, and study the information in the picture. Then, read questions 1 to 9 and answer them.

101 **DALMATIANS** is a fantastic comedy.

The story takes place in and around London. The main characters are: Cruella De Vil, an evil fashion designer; Roger and Anita, a kind couple; their two Dalmatians, Pongo and Perdy; and, of course, the adorable puppies.

Cruella is a horrible woman! She wants to make a coat from the fur of Dalmatian puppies. She orders her two assistants to steal Pongo and Perdy's puppies. The assistants take them to an old house and keep them with some other stolen Dalmatian puppies. Pongo and Perdy decide to save the puppies and their adventure begins.

101 DALMATIANS is an amusing film for the whole family! Don't miss it!

101 DALMATIANS

Director: Stephen Herek
Cast: Glenn Close, Jeff Daniels, Joely Richardson

Home Alone

Questions

1 What type of film is *101 DALMATIANS*?
2 Who is the director?
3 Who is in the cast?
4 Where does the story take place?
5 Who are the main characters?
6 What does Cruella want to make?
7 Who steals Pongo and Perdy's puppies?
8 Where do they take them?
9 What does Tom think about the film?

3 **Match the words to their definitions.**

1 cast ————— a husband and wife

2 take place b baby dog

3 main character c animal's coat

4 fashion designer d helper

5 couple e happen

6 puppy f take sth that isn't yours

7 fur ——→ g actors and actresses in a film

8 order h most important person in a book, film, etc

9 assistant i person who designs clothes

10 steal j command

4 **Match the adjectives in the list to their synonyms.**

wicked, awful, great, lovable, funny, friendly

1 a **fantastic** comedy = ...
2 an **evil** fashion designer = ...
3 a **kind** couple = ...
4 **adorable** puppies = ...
5 a **horrible** woman = ...
6 an **amusing** film = ...

STUDY TIP

• We can form some **adjectives** by adding **-ing** to the base form of the verb.
 e.g. **excite → exciting, amuse → amusing**

• We use these adjectives to describe **what somebody or something is like**.
 *e.g. 101 DALMATIANS is an **amusing** film.*
  *(What is the film like? It's **amusing**.)*

5 **Use the verbs in brackets to form adjectives, as in the example.**

1 We really enjoyed ourselves because it was a very ...*entertaining*... film. **(entertain)**

2 *20,000 Leagues Under the Sea* is a very .... book. **(interest)**

3 The film was very ...., so I fell asleep. **(bore)**

4 I finished the book in one evening because it was a very .... story. **(thrill)**

5 Many people thought the director's new film was .... **(disappoint)**

6 The little boy watched a .... film on TV last night, so he couldn't sleep. **(frighten)**

7 *Star Wars* is an .... science-fiction film. Don't miss it! **(amaze)**

8 It was a .... story about a boy's difficult life. **(touch)**

6 **Use the adjectives from Ex. 5 to write sentences about films you have seen, as in the example.**

*e.g. Die Hard II is a **thrilling** film.*

....
....
....
....
....
....
....
....
....

41

Lights! Camera! ACTION!

7 Use the key and the information about the films below to: a) complete the paragraph about *The Lost World: Jurassic Park*; b) write similar paragraphs for the other films.

KEY: touching   amusing   exciting   boring

Type of Film: Action

Place: Costa Rica

Main Characters: the scientists, Dr Ian Malcolm and Dr Sarah Harding; the wicked hunter, Roland Tembo; and the frightening dinosaurs

The Lost World: Jurassic Park is an *exciting* action film. The story takes place in .... The main characters are the scientists, ... and .... ; the ...., Roland Tembo; and, of course, ...

Type of Film: Cartoon

Place: America

Main Characters: the American Indian princess, Pocahontas; Captain John Smith; Chief Powhatan; and John Ratcliffe, the evil Governor

Type of Film: Romance

Place: Florida

Main Characters: Romeo and Juliet, the young couple in love

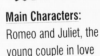

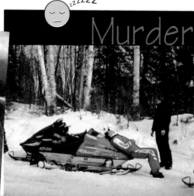

Type of Film: Horror

Place: Austria

Main Characters: John Lawless; his friend, Mark; and Phil, John's brother

8 Look at the phrases below and put a tick (✓) in the column they belong to.

	♥	✗
Don't waste your time watching this film.		
Don't miss it!		
It's a must!		
Don't bother with this one.		
I definitely recommend it.		

9 a) Use a suitable phrase from Ex. 8 to give recommendations for the following films.

1 *Murder* is a boring film. *Don't bother with this one.*

2 *Romeo and Juliet* is a very touching film. ....

3 *Pocahontas* is an amusing cartoon for the whole family. ....

4 *The Lost World: Jurassic Park* is an exciting film. ....

b) Use the phrases above to talk about some films you have seen.

STUDY TIP

- We use the **present simple** when we write reviews for films, books and plays.
  e.g. *The story **begins** when Sarah **meets** Tom.*
- We join sentences using **and** (similar ideas), **so** (result) and **because** (reason).
  e.g. *He leaves Paris **and** goes to London.*
  e.g. *He hasn't got a bicycle **so** he borrows his friend's.*
  e.g. *He sells his car **because** he needs the money.*

42

10 Read the following extract from a film review and fill in *and*, *so* or *because*.

Popeye goes to Sweethaven **1)** .... he wants to find his father. There, he meets Olive Oyl **2)** .... they fall in love. After a while, they find a little boy, Swee' Pea, **3)** .... take him home. Bluto also loves Olive, **4)** ...., one day, he kidnaps her. Bluto takes Olive to his house **5)** .... locks her in a room. Popeye decides to save her **6)** .... the adventure begins.

11 Read the questions below, then read the dialogue and fill in the missing questions.

- Who is ET?
- What is the plot of the film?
- How does ET feel?
- Who are the main characters?
- What happens then?
- Where does the story take place?
- What happens in the end?

Bobby: I saw a great science-fiction film on TV last night: *ET The Extra-Terrestrial*.
Kelly: Really! **1)** ....
Bobby: In a small town in America.
Kelly: I see. **2)** ....
Bobby: Well, there is Elliott, a young boy; Mike and Gertie, his brother and sister; and, of course, ET.
Kelly: **3)** ....
Bobby: ET is a lovable creature from outer space.
Kelly: Mm, it sounds interesting. **4)** ....
....
Bobby: Well, Elliott finds ET when the other aliens leave Earth without him.
Kelly: **5)** ....
Bobby: Elliott takes ET to his house to hide him. He takes care of ET, together with his brother and sister. They also teach him things about life on Earth.
Kelly: **6)** ....
Bobby: Well, ET loves his new friends, but he misses his family and wants to return home.
Kelly: That's sweet. **7)** ....
Bobby: The children find a way to help him return home.
Kelly: Wow! It sounds like a great film!
Bobby: It is! You must see it!

WRITING

12 Use the information from Ex. 11, the plan below and the picture from the Photo File section, to write a film review (80-100 words) for your school newspaper about *ET The Extra-Terrestrial*. Also use the text of Ex. 2 as a model.

Director: Steven Spielberg
Cast: Henry Thomas, Robert MacNaughton, Drew Barrymore

Plan

Paragraph 1: name and type of film
↓
Paragraph 2: where the story takes place; main characters
↓
Paragraph 3: main events of plot in chronological order
↓
Paragraph 4: your opinion and recommendations

Take my Advice

1 a) Match the words to the pictures.

1 ☐ passport   3 ☐ luggage
2 ☐ German marks   4 ☐ airport

b) The following sentences give advice to someone who is going to travel by plane from England to Frankfurt. Read the sentences and fill in the correct word(s) from the list above.

1 You must arrive at the .... at least one hour before your flight.

2 You must take your .... with you.

3 You should change some pounds into .... before you go.

4 You should make sure your .... is under twenty kilos.

2 Read the letter below, then read the sentences and underline the correct words in bold.

18 Morton Road
Oxford
OX4 3LL
23rd April, ...

Dear Karen,

Thanks for your letter. Frankfurt is a great choice for your holiday. Since this is your first holiday abroad, here is some useful advice.

First of all, you must take your passport with you. You can't travel abroad without it! Also, you must arrive at the airport at least one hour before your flight leaves. You need time to check in.

Of course, you should keep your luggage under twenty kilos, because airline companies charge extra for heavy luggage. Finally, you should also change some pounds into German marks before you go. You need money to spend when you get there.

Anyway, that's enough from me! Have a lovely trip and don't forget to send me a postcard!

Lots of love,
Claire

1 You must take your **passport** / **visa** with you.

2 You must arrive at the airport **one** / **three** hour(s) before your flight.

3 You should keep your luggage **under** / **over** twenty kilos.

4 You should change some pounds into **dollars** / **German marks** before you go.

5 Don't **remember** / **forget** to send me a postcard.

3 Fill in the words from the list below.

charge, great, useful, trip, check, companies, travel, heavy

1 a .... choice
2 to .... abroad
3 .... advice
4 to .... in
5 airline ....
6 to .... extra
7 .... luggage
8 a lovely ....

STUDY TIP

• We use **should**/**shouldn't** to **give advice**; i.e. to say what would be a good/bad idea for someone to do.
  *e.g. You **should** keep your luggage under twenty kilos.*
  (= It would be a good idea.)
  *You **shouldn't** eat a lot of chocolate.*

• We use **must**/**mustn't** to **give strong advice**; i.e. to tell someone what it is absolutely necessary to do.
  *e.g. You **must** take your passport with you.*
  (= It is absolutely necessary/I strongly recommend)
  *You **mustn't** drink and drive.*

---

4 Read Claire's letter again. What does she think is a good idea for Karen to do? What does she think is absolutely necessary for Karen to do?

5 Jake is going to London on holiday. Match the useful tips to their reasons, then make sentences giving advice to Jake, using to, as in the example.

Useful Tips	Reasons
1 take an umbrella	a make sure you don't get lost
2 bring your camera	b protect yourself from the rain
3 buy a map	c keep yourself warm
4 pack some jumpers	d take pictures of the sights

*e.g. You **should** take an umbrella **to** protect yourself from the rain.*

---

6 Bob is flying to Paris. Match the useful tips to their reasons, then use because to make sentences, as in the example.

Strong Advice	Reasons
1 not take animals on the plane	a they can affect planes' computers
2 not smoke on the plane	b many of them carry diseases
3 not use mobile phones on the plane	c you can't get on the plane without it
4 take your plane ticket	d cigarettes can cause fires

*e.g. You **mustn't** take animals on the plane **because** many of them carry diseases.*

STUDY TIP

We use the **imperative** and the **negative imperative** for **written warnings**.
*e.g. **Keep** off the grass.   **Don't feed** the animals.*

---

7 Match the signs to the warnings, then explain what each sign means using must or mustn't.

| 1 | c | | 2 | | 3 | |

a Don't swim here.
b Drive slowly.
c Don't smoke here.
d Stop here.
e Don't litter.
f Don't turn right.
g Don't park here.
h Do not enter.

| 4 | | 5 | |

| 6 | | 7 | | 8 | |

*1 c - You **mustn't** smoke here.* ....
....
....
....

45

8 Match the prompts to the pictures below, then make sentences to give advice to parents using must/mustn't, as in the example.

a let children near the cooker when it is on
b leave knives on the table
c watch children while they are playing
d keep all medicines in high cupboards
e let children play with matches
f cover all sockets

1 *You **mustn't** leave knives on the table.*

2 ....
....

3 ....
....

4 ....
....

5 ....
....

6 ....
....

9 **a)** Chris is sixteen years old and he is planning to go camping for the first time with some friends. He wrote a letter to the park director asking for information. Read the letter Chris received from him. In which paragraph does the park director give strong advice?

Dear Chris,

Thanks for your interest in our park. Here are some tips to help you and your friends with your camping trip.

First of all, you must bring a tent and sleeping bag, because Grizedale National Park does not provide them. Also, when you light a camp fire, you must always put it out before you go to sleep, to avoid forest fires. Keep in mind that you mustn't play loud music, because the noise disturbs the other campers. Of course, you mustn't leave any rubbish behind, because it harms the environment.

You should also bring a torch to help you see in the dark, and insect repellent to protect yourself from mosquitoes. Finally, you shouldn't forget to pack a jumper to keep you warm on chilly evenings.

Keep these tips in mind and you shouldn't have any problems. I hope you have a nice trip.

Yours,
William Peterson

b) Read the letter again and complete the table below. Then, use the notes to give advice to Chris. Use **to** or **because**.

Must/Mustn't	Reasons
• bring a tent and sleeping bag	• ....
•	• avoid forest fires
• not play loud music	• ....
•	• it harms the environment

Should/Shouldn't	Reasons
•	• help you see in the dark
• bring insect repellent	• ....
•	• keep you warm on chilly evenings

10 Rewrite the sentences using should, shouldn't, must or mustn't.

1 I strongly advise you to keep your passport in a safe place.

You must keep your passport in a safe place.

2 It would be a good idea to visit your doctor before you leave.

You should visit your doctor before you leave.

3 It wouldn't be a good idea to drink alcohol.

....

4 I strongly advise you not to eat fatty foods before you fly.

....

5 It would be a good idea to use traveller's cheques.

....

6 I strongly advise you not to wear expensive jewellery.

....

7 It would be a good idea to book a hotel before you leave.

....

8 I strongly advise you to drink bottled water.

....

11 James is travelling around Europe by car. Look at the table below and match each piece of advice to the reason. Then, make sentences using to or because.

Must/Mustn't	Reasons
1 buy a road map	**a** there is always a danger of accidents
2 take a first aid kit with you	**b** you can cause an accident
3 check the car engine	**c** help you find your way
4 exceed the speed limit	**d** make sure it is in good condition

Should/Shouldn't	Reasons
5 drive on the main roads	**e** it is dangerous
6 listen to the weather forecast	**f** avoid getting lost
7 not travel alone	**g** find out what clothes you need to take

WRITING

12 Use the information in Ex. 11, the paragraph plan below and the beginning and ending given, to complete the letter to James from his friend Bill (60 - 80 words). Use the letter in Ex. 2 as a model.

Plan

40 Redhill Road
Sydney 2001
New South Wales
Australia
24th May, ...

Dear James,

Paragraph 1: *Nice to hear from you again! I went on a similar trip around Europe five years ago - it was great! Here are some tips to help you with your trip.*

Paragraphs 2-3: advice and reasons

Paragraph 4: *Keep these tips in mind and you shouldn't have any problems. Hope to hear from you soon.*

Yours,
Bill

A Red Rag to a Bull!

1 a) **Look at the pictures and fill in the correct numbers in the boxes below.**

1	Bernie the bull	□ gate	□ Jeff Monk	□ bucket
□	trousers	□ horns	□ Jeff's wife	

b) **Match each picture to one of the following sentences.**

1 Jeff's wife laughed when she saw him without his trousers.

Picture ....

2 Jeff dropped his bucket and ran as fast as he could.

Picture ....

3 He had a lot of animals, but his favourite was a bull called Bernie.

Picture ....

4 Then, he threw Jeff up into the air.

Picture ....

2 **First, put the verbs in the list into the *past simple*, then read the story below and fill in the gaps with the correct verb.**

laugh, have, say, run, shout, put ... on, call, drop, live, buy

A Red Rag To a Bull!

Jeff Monk **1)** .... on a quiet farm in the country. He **2)** .... a lot of animals, but his favourite was a bull called Bernie. Bernie was almost three years old and everyone **3)** .... , "Be careful near him, Jeff. Bulls can be dangerous." Jeff didn't listen to them, though. Bernie was like a friend to him.

On Jeff's birthday, his wife **4)** .... him an expensive red shirt. Jeff **5)** .... it .... and went out to feed Bernie, as usual. He went to the field next to the house and **6)** .... him, "Come on, boy! Time to eat!" Bernie looked up and suddenly gave a loud snort. Next, he began to run angrily towards Jeff. Jeff **7)** .... his bucket and ran as fast as he could. He **8)** .... loudly to his wife, "Help! Help!"

Jeff ran to the gate, but before he could climb over it, Bernie's long horns hooked onto Jeff's trousers. Then, he threw Jeff up into the air. Fortunately, Jeff's trousers came off, so he managed to get free. He **9)** .... quickly to the house.

Jeff's wife **10)** .... when she saw him without his trousers. "Well, at least your new shirt is okay," she said. "Next time don't wear it to feed Bernie!"

3 Read the story again and complete the questions for the underlined words, as in the example.

e.g. Who lived on a quiet farm in the country?
Jeff Monk lived on a quiet farm in the country.

1 What ....?
Jeff's favourite animal was a bull.

2 How ....?
Bernie was almost three years old.

3 What ....?
Jeff's wife bought him an expensive red shirt.

4 Why ....?
Jeff went to the field to feed Bernie.

5 Who ....?
Bernie began to run angrily towards Jeff.

6 What ....?
Jeff dropped his bucket and ran as fast as he could.

7 What ....?
Jeff shouted loudly to his wife, "Help! Help!"

8 Where ....?
Jeff ran to the gate.

9 What ....?
Bernie threw Jeff up into the air.

10 What ....
when she saw him without his trousers?
Jeff's wife laughed when she saw him without his trousers.

4 Read the summary of the story below and correct the parts that are underlined, as in the example.

e.g. 1 Jeff Monk didn't live in a flat in the country.
He lived on a quiet farm in the country.

Jeff Monk lived **1)** in a flat in the country. He had **2)** a few animals, but his favourite was **3)** a horse called Bernie. On Jeff's birthday, his wife bought him **4)** a cheap blue shirt. Jeff put it on and went into the field to feed Bernie. Bernie looked up and gave a **5)** quiet snort. Then, he ran **6)** happily towards Jeff. Jeff ran to the gate, but Bernie's long horns hooked onto Jeff's trousers. Jeff's trousers came off and he managed to get free. His wife **7)** shouted when she saw him without his trousers.

5 What's the word?

1 not safe = ... **gandesuro**

2 to give food = to .... **edef**

3 a noise through the nose = a .... **rnots**

4 what we like most = our .... **rafuvoeit**

6 Underline the correct prepositions in bold.

1 Sally went to the circus **on / in** her birthday.

2 It's cold outside, so put your coat **off / on**.

3 When he looked **on / up**, he saw an aeroplane.

4 The boys climbed **over / through** the wall.

5 The little girl ran **up / towards** her mother.

6 The horse was like a friend **to / by** Rachel.

7 Gary threw the ball **along / into** the air.

8 It was windy and his hat came **off / out**.

STUDY TIP

When we write a **story**, we use **adjectives** to make the story more interesting. **Adjectives** describe **nouns**.
*e.g. His wife bought him an **expensive red** shirt.*

---

7 Replace the adjectives in bold with similar ones from the list, as in the example.

tasty, scary, pretty, cheerful, horrible, huge

1 Ann cooked a **delicious** meal for dinner. ..... *tasty* ....

2 Mrs Brown bought a **beautiful** dress .... for the party.

3 He sent a **large** bouquet of flowers to .... his wife.

4 The children watched a **frightening** film .... on TV last night.

5 I had a **terrible** experience during my .... holiday last year.

6 Bob looked at me with a **happy** smile .... on his face.

STUDY TIP

• When we write a story, we also use **adverbs**. We can form **adverbs from some adjectives** by adding **-ly**.
*e.g. sudden - sudden**ly**, fortunate - fortunate**ly***

• **Adverbs** describe **verbs**.
*e.g. She **sang** the song **beautifully**.*
*(How did she sing the song? **Beautifully**.)*

• **Note:** Some adverbs don't follow the rule above.
*e.g. good - **well**, fast - **fast**, hard - **hard***

---

8 Fill in the correct adverb.

1 I smiled at him .... (**cheerful**).

2 The boy ran away .... (**quick**).

3 I .... (**slow**) got up from my seat.

4 Just then, the telephone rang .... (**loud**).

5 Sarah did .... (**bad**) in her exams.

6 I listened .... (**careful**) to the news on the radio.

49

9 Fill in the gaps with an appropriate adverb from the list.

beautifully, well, wickedly, carefully, loudly, quickly

We looked at the man
1) .... "Look! It's Bobbie Batter, the famous singer!" my friend Jenny shouted 2) .... "Let's talk to him!" Bobbie saw Jenny coming towards him and ran 3) .... into the restaurant.

The next moment, he crashed into a table and fell onto the floor. "He can sing 4) .... , but he can't see very 5) .... !" we laughed 6) ....

STUDY TIP

When we write stories, we can use **somebody's exact words** (Direct Speech) to make our story more **dramatic**. When we write somebody's exact words, we use **inverted commas**.
e.g. **"Come on, boy! Time to eat!"**

---

10 Read the speech bubbles below and use them to fill in the gaps in the sentences.

1 Suddenly, the branch snapped and Alex fell.
   "....................." he screamed, but just then his shirt ...
2 Beth was in bed when her mother came into her room.
   ".." her mother said cheerfully.
3 ".." said the teacher.
   Then, he gave us our tests.
4 She sat down and the waiter walked towards her.
   ".." he asked politely.

STUDY TIP

When we write stories, we can use **similes (like + noun)** to make our stories more interesting.
*e.g. Bernie was **like a friend** to Jeff.*

11 First, match the verbs to the nouns to make similes. Then, use them to fill in the gaps in the sentences that follow.

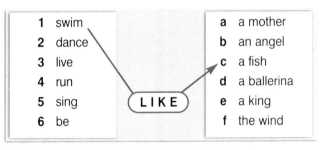

1 swim	a a mother
2 dance	b an angel
3 live	c a fish
4 run	d a ballerina
5 sing	e a king
6 be	f the wind

1 Little Mary sang .... in the school play last week.
2 Tom could swim .... when he was only two years old.
3 Pam turned on the radio and danced around the room ....
4 Elvis Presley was very rich and lived .... in Graceland.
5 The man came out of the bank and ran .... up the street.
6 The nurse looked after Freddy very well. She was .... to him.

12 Study the examples below, then join the sentences with and, but or so.

e.g.   *Jeff put his shirt on. He went out to feed Bernie.*
   *Jeff put his shirt on **and** went out to feed Bernie.*
   Jeff's trousers came off. He managed to get free.
   *Jeff's trousers came off, **so** he managed to get free.*
   He had a lot of animals. His favourite was a bull.
   *He had a lot of animals, **but** his favourite was a bull.*

1 It was a warm sunny day. We decided to go on a picnic.
   ....
2 We got our things ready. We put them in the car.
   ....
3 Simon tried to start the car. Smoke began to come out of the engine.
   ....
4 We jumped out quickly. We ran to get a fire extinguisher.
   ....
5 The door was locked. We couldn't get into the house.
   ....

6 One of the windows was open. Simon climbed into the house.

....

7 Our dog thought Simon was a thief. He bit his leg.

....

8 Simon was alright in the end. We didn't go on a picnic that day!

....

13 a) **Read the following story and correct the mistakes.**

Tony's uncle, Don, lived in a small village in the mountains. One day, Tony decided to visit him. The snow was very deep, so Tony couldn't walked fast. Suddenly, he heared a strange sound. It was like a babys cry.

Tony looked around and saw a huge white dog. At first, he thinked the dog was hungry, but then he saw a red shape in the snow. Tony run quickly towards the dog.

The dog started to bark. "What is it, boy?" Tony asked. "What has you got there?" Tony looked closely at the red shape. It was a young woman, but she couldn't move. "My leg," she said quietly. "Please help me!"

Tony ran for help, and soon the girl was in a warm hospital bed. Tony was glad. He had two new freinds now – Lucy, and her brave dog, lucky!

b) **Read the story in Ex. 13 again and find the adjectives and the adverbs in it. Which nouns/verbs do they describe?**

• **Adjectives:** *small (village),* ....
....
....

• **Adverbs:** *(walk) fast,* ....
....
....

14 **Read this interview with Josh Bell for the magazine *Summer Fun*, and put the verbs in brackets into the past simple.**

J: Last summer, I **1)** .... **(work)** as a lifeguard on a very popular beach. On my first day there, I **2)** .... **(feel)** a little anxious. It **3)** .... **(be)** a hot sunny day, so there were a lot of people in the water.

R: So, what happened?

J: Suddenly, I **4)** .... **(see)** a large grey shape in the sea. I **5)** .... **(panic)** and **6)** .... **(tell)** everyone to get out of the water. They all **7)** .... **(begin)** to swim quickly to the shore.

R: What happened next?

J: The lifeboat crew **8)** .... **(speed)** out immediately to check that everything was alright. Five minutes later, they **9)** .... **(come)** back. One of the crew **10)** .... **(hold)** something up for me to see. He **11)** .... **(have)** a grey surfboard in his hands!

R: A surfboard! It wasn't a shark then?

J: No! I felt silly, but at least no one was hurt!

15 **Use the information in Ex. 14 to answer the questions in the plan below. Then, use the completed plan, the pictures and the beginning given in the Photo File section, to write a story (100-150 words) which ends with these words:**

Josh felt silly, but at least no one was hurt!

Plan

Paragraph 1:	mention the time, place and people involved

When did the story happen?
Where did Josh work as a lifeguard?
How did Josh feel on his first day?
What was the weather like?

Paragraphs 2-3:	develop the story

What did Josh suddenly see?
How did he react? What did he do?
What did the swimmers do?

What did the lifeboat crew do? Why?
When did they come back?
What did one of the crew do? Why?
What did he have in his hands?

Paragraph 4:	describe what happened in the end and people's feelings

Going North

THE LITTLE MERMAID

2

TIVOLI

3

4

GAMMEL STRAND

AMALIENBORG PALACE

1

THE NYHAVN CANAL

5

1 Look at the pictures. Which shows:

an amusement park?	..3..	a guard?	....
an antiques market?	....	a canal?	....
people on a boat trip?	....	a palace?	....
a statue of a mermaid?	....	a brewery?	....

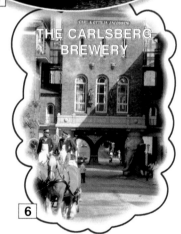

THE CARLSBERG BREWERY

6

2 Melanie is going on holiday. Read the letter she sent to her friend, then read questions 1 to 5 and answer them.

219 Astor Street
London
SW7 LY3

20th May, ...

Dear Rosie,

I've got some great news! I am finally going on the holiday of my dreams. I'm spending the first two weeks of June in the wonderful city of Copenhagen. Isn't that exciting?

I'm flying there on Monday morning, 2nd June. First, I'm going to see the beautiful statue of the Little Mermaid. Then, I'm going to see the changing of the guard at Amalienborg Palace. I'm also going to Tivoli to go on the rides. It's one of the most famous amusement parks in the world! I am definitely not going to miss the chance to go on a boat trip on the Nyhavn Canal to see more of Copenhagen. Finally, I'm going to visit the antiques market on Gammel Strand to buy some souvenirs, and the Carlsberg Brewery to see how they make beer.

I'm really excited because I know it's going to be an amazing holiday! Hope to hear from you soon.

Love,
Melanie

1 Where is Melanie going?
2 How long is she going to stay there?
3 When is she going on holiday?
4 What is she going to do there?
5 How does she feel about her holiday?

3 Fill in the correct word from the list below.

antiques, holiday, guard, amusement, buy, boat

1 the .... 4 the changing of the
  of my dreams ....
2 a(n)...................... park 5 a(n) .... trip
3 to .... souvenirs 6 a(n) .... market

4 Read Melanie's letter again, then fill in the adjectives from the list below. Finally, use the phrases to make sentences.

famous, great, beautiful, wonderful

1 .... news 3 a ....
2 the .... amusement park
  city of Copenhagen 4 a .... statue

5 Helen is going to London. Look at the table showing her plans and arrangements, then make sentences using the present continuous or be going to, as in the example.

	PLANS	ARRANGEMENTS
fly to London tomorrow		✓
visit Trafalgar Square	✓	
stay at the Savoy Hotel		✓
see Big Ben	✓	
rent a car	✓	
visit the British Museum	✓	
come back 2nd July		✓

*e.g. Helen **is flying** to London tomorrow.*

STUDY TIP

We use the **to - infinitive** (infinitive of purpose) to give the reason why we do something.
*e.g. I am going to visit Amalienborg Palace **to see** the changing of the guard.*

6 Read Melanie's letter again. Fill in the reasons why she is going to visit the places in the list below, then make sentences, as in the example.

Places	Reasons
Amalienborg Palace	*to see the changing of the guard*
Tivoli	....
antiques market	....
Carlsberg Brewery	....

e.g. She is going to visit Amalienborg Palace to see the changing of the guard.

7 Match the plans to the reasons, then make sentences, as in the example.

Plans	Reasons
1 visit the gallery	a enjoy the interesting sights
2 find a nice restaurant	b see a play
3 go to the antiques market	c have lunch
4 visit the Royal Theatre	d buy some souvenirs
5 go on a boat trip	e admire the paintings

e.g. I am going to visit the gallery to admire the paintings.

8 Steve is going to Prague. Fill in the gaps with adjectives from the list below, then underline the reason why Steve is going to visit each place.

relaxing, historic, fascinating, lovely, famous, delicious

Prague

I am going to Charles Bridge to enjoy the **1)** ... *lovely* ... view.

I am going to the **2)** .... Prague Castle to take some pictures.

I am going to the National Gallery to admire the **3)** .... paintings and statues.

I am going to take a **4)** .... boat trip on the Vltava to see more of Prague.

I am going to visit the Old Town Square to see the **5)** .... medieval clock.

I'm going to Wenceslas Square to have a cup of coffee and some **6)** .... pancakes.

9 a) Read Jane's letter about her trip to Rome and expand the notes in the second paragraph into full sentences. Use first, then, also and finally in your paragraph.

Fontana di Trevi

522 Corey Drive
London
SW1 3BF

10th August, ...

Dear Mark,

Guess what! I am going on a school trip to Rome for a week! Can you believe it?

- fly there / Wednesday 20th September / afternoon ....
- visit the Colosseum and the Roman Forum / admire the ancient temples and monuments ....
- go to the famous Fontana di Trevi / throw a coin in and make a wish ....
- visit the Piazza di Spagna / see the artists ....
- walk along the famous Via Veneto / do some window shopping ....

I am so thrilled about this trip! It's going to be absolutely fabulous! Bye for now.

Love,
Jane

b) Read the letter again and answer these questions.

1 Whose address is at the top of the letter?
2 How does Jane begin her letter?
3 What does Jane mention in the first paragraph?
4 What is the second paragraph about?
5 What is the third paragraph about?
6 How does Jane end her letter?

WRITING

10 a) You are going on a trip to Paris for two weeks. Read the prompts under the pictures, then make sentences with the *to-infinitive*.

b) Choose five of the sights and write a letter to a friend about what you are going to do in Paris (**100 - 120 words**). Use the paragraph plan given and the letter in Ex. 2 as a model.

5 go to the Left Bank / have a cup of coffee and a croissant

6 book a table at Maxim's / taste some delicious French dishes

7 visit Versailles / walk around the palace and its beautiful gardens

1 go to the Eiffel Tower / enjoy the spectacular view of the city

2 visit the famous Notre Dame Cathedral / take pictures

Plan

(Your address)
....
....
....
(Date)

Dear (+ *your friend's first name*),

Paragraph 1: reason for writing, (where you are going, how long you are staying there)

Paragraph 2: your fixed arrangements and plans/intentions

Paragraph 3: how you feel and closing remarks

Love,
(your first name)

3 spend a day at the Louvre / look at the wonderful paintings and statues

4 go on a boat trip on the Seine / see more of Paris

Getting Ready

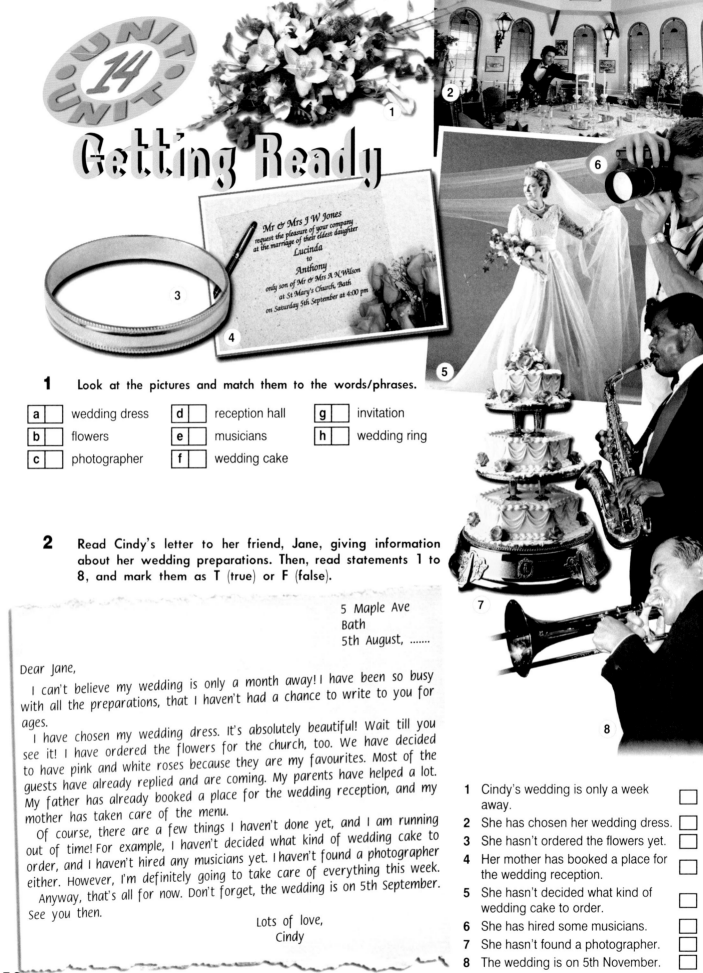

Mr & Mrs J W Jones
request the pleasure of your company
at the marriage of their eldest daughter
Lucinda
to
Anthony
only son of Mr & Mrs A N Wilson
at St Mary's Church, Bath
on Saturday 5th September at 4:00 pm

1 Look at the pictures and match them to the words/phrases.

a		wedding dress	d		reception hall	g		invitation
b		flowers	e		musicians	h		wedding ring
c		photographer	f		wedding cake			

2 Read Cindy's letter to her friend, Jane, giving information about her wedding preparations. Then, read statements 1 to 8, and mark them as **T** (true) or **F** (false).

5 Maple Ave
Bath
5th August, ...

Dear Jane,

I can't believe my wedding is only a month away! I have been so busy with all the preparations, that I haven't had a chance to write to you for ages.

I have chosen my wedding dress. It's absolutely beautiful! Wait till you see it! I have ordered the flowers for the church, too. We have decided to have pink and white roses because they are my favourites. Most of the guests have already replied and are coming. My parents have helped a lot. My father has already booked a place for the wedding reception, and my mother has taken care of the menu.

Of course, there are a few things I haven't done yet, and I am running out of time! For example, I haven't decided what kind of wedding cake to order, and I haven't hired any musicians yet. I haven't found a photographer either. However, I'm definitely going to take care of everything this week.

Anyway, that's all for now. Don't forget, the wedding is on 5th September. See you then.

Lots of love,
Cindy

1 Cindy's wedding is only a week away. ☐
2 She has chosen her wedding dress. ☐
3 She hasn't ordered the flowers yet. ☐
4 Her mother has booked a place for the wedding reception. ☐
5 She hasn't decided what kind of wedding cake to order. ☐
6 She has hired some musicians. ☐
7 She hasn't found a photographer. ☐
8 The wedding is on 5th November. ☐

3 Fill in the gaps with words from the list.

busy, time, all, chance, ages, book, care

1 to have a .... to do sth
2 for ....
3 to be ....
4 to take .... of sth
5 to .... a place for the wedding reception
6 to run out of ....
7 that's .... for now

---

4 Read the letter again and underline the present perfect forms. Which of the past participles are regular, and which are irregular?

5 Fill in the past participle of these verbs.

1	write	....	10	drink	....
2	be	....	11	eat	....
3	tell	....	12	pack	....
4	send	....	13	give	....
5	think	....	14	go	....
6	boil	....	15	leave	....
7	buy	....	16	make	....
8	see	....	17	take	....
9	come	....	18	organise	....

6 Peter is organising a picnic. Look at his list and make sentences about what he has already done and what he hasn't done yet.

- Peter **has already bought** orange juice and snacks.
- Peter **hasn't roasted** the chicken **yet**.
- ....
- ....
- ....
- ....
- ....

Picnic List

Buy orange juice/snacks. ✓
Roast the chicken. ✗
Boil some eggs. ✓
Make a salad. ✗
Pack the picnic basket. ✗
Put a blanket in the car. ✗
Check the weather forecast. ✓

Getting Ready

7 Put the verbs in brackets into the present perfect.

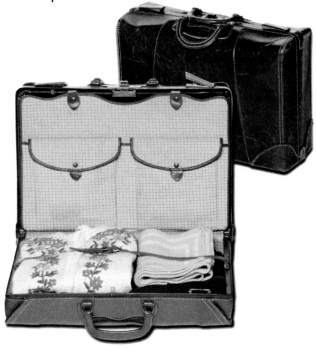

1 A: .... **(you / pack)** all your suitcases yet?

   B: No, I .... **(not / have)** time to pack all of them.

2 A: .... **(you / order)** the food for your party yet?

   B: Yes, I .... **(decide)** to order some pizzas.

3 A: What .... **(he / do)** about the evening's entertainment?

   B: He .... **(hire)** a jazz band.

4 A: .... **(she / send)** all the invitations yet?

   B: No, she hasn't, because she .... **(be)** very busy.

8 Underline the correct time expressions.

1 Paul has **already** / **yet** cleaned the house.
2 He hasn't visited London **for** / **since** he was fifteen years old.
3 I have **never** / **ever** seen such a beautiful wedding dress.
4 She has **just** / **so far** left for the airport.
5 Have you **never** / **ever** tried Chinese food?
6 We have worked for this company **for** / **since** many years.
7 Has she baked the cake **yet** / **just**?
8 I have written three letters **ever** / **so far** today.

9 Judy and Mark have bought a new house. Look at the prompts and make sentences, as in the example.

e.g. They have already packed their things in boxes.

> pack their things in boxes ✓
> book a removal van ✗
> tell their friends their new address ✓
> clean their new house ✗
> buy some new furniture ✓
> walk around their new neighbourhood ✗
> buy some new curtains ✓

....
....
....
....
....
....

WRITING

TIP

When we write a **letter** to a friend telling him/her about our **preparations for an event** (such as a party, wedding, celebration, etc), we divide it into four paragraphs.

• We **begin** by stating **why we are writing** the letter.
• In the **second paragraph**, we write about the **preparations we have already made**.
• In the **third paragraph**, we mention the **preparations we haven't made yet**.
• We **end** our letter by reminding our friend about the **date of the event**. We include a **closing remark**.
  e.g. That's all for now. I hope you can be there.
We use the **present perfect** to talk about the preparations we have / haven't made.

10 **a)** Read Emily's letter to Fred and put the paragraphs in the correct order.

22 Park Lane
Middleton
10th June, ...

Dear Fred,

A ☐ We have completed most of the preparations, but there are still some things we haven't done yet. For example, we haven't sold all the tickets and we haven't found anyone to do our make-up. However, we are going to take care of all that this week.

B ☐ Here's my latest news about the biggest event of the school year — our production of the famous musical, *Grease*.

C ☐ Remember, the opening night is on Saturday 25th June at 7:30 pm. I hope you can be there!

D ☐ You can't imagine who I'm playing — Sandy, the main female character! Isn't that great? Anyway, we have all learnt our lines and we have also tried on our costumes. They look fantastic! The rehearsals have been a lot of fun, especially now that we have learned the songs and the dance routines. My classmates have also done an amazing job with the stage props. Wait till you see them!

Love,
Emily

b) **Which paragraph includes:**

a) the preparations they haven't made yet?   The .... paragraph.

b) the closing remarks and the date of the event?   The .... paragraph.

c) the reason why Emily has written the letter?   The .... paragraph.

d) the preparations they have already completed?   The .... paragraph.

11 Use the prompts and the paragraph plan to write a letter to a friend giving information about your birthday party (**70 - 100** words). Use the letter in **Ex. 2** as a model. You can start the first paragraph like this:

Sorry I haven't written for ages, but I have been very busy with all the preparations for my birthday party ...

phone my friends	✔
buy everything I need for the barbecue	✔
order a cake	✘
borrow some CDs	✔
buy a film for my camera	✘

Plan

(Your address and date)

Dear (+ your friend's first name),

Paragraph 1: reason for writing
⬇
Paragraph 2: preparations you have already made
⬇
Paragraph 3: preparations you haven't made yet
⬇
Paragraph 4: date of event and closing remarks

Lots of love/Best wishes, etc
(your first name)

59

Whatever Will Be, Will Be!

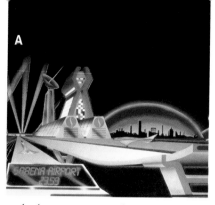

1   Which picture shows:

[1] a child using a computer?   [4] a colony on another planet?

[2] a robot?   [5] a spaceship?

[3] some planets?   [6] a building made of metal and glass?

2   Will **and** won't **are used to:**

a talk about plans and intentions.
b talk about fixed arrangements.

c make predictions about the future.

3   **What will life be like in the year 2200? Use the prompts below to make predictions about the future, as in the example.**

children / use books - computers
people / travel by aeroplane - by spaceship
people / only live on Earth - also in colonies on other planets
people / live in small houses - in tall buildings made of metal and glass
people / only travel to other countries - also to other planets

e.g. **In my opinion** *children* **won't** *use books. They* **will** *use computers.*

4   **a) Read the following magazine article about what life in the year 2200 will be like, and fill in the topic sentences a to c.**

FORWARD TO THE FUTURE!

1 ....
Will it be better or worse? In my opinion, it will certainly be a lot more fun.

2 ....
....
There won't be any classrooms or teachers because children will learn at home with computers. Space travel will be cheap, so people will use spaceships to visit other planets. People will live in tall buildings made of metal and glass. Also, they won't use petrol or gas, so there won't be much pollution. What is more, people will be healthier because there will be cures for all diseases. Finally, people will have more free time because robots will do all the boring jobs, such as cooking and cleaning.

3 ....
Positive changes will make it possible for people to enjoy their lives more.

a) There will be drastic changes in education, transport, housing, the environment, health and lifestyles.
b) In conclusion, I believe life in the year 2200 will be better.
c) Life in the year 2200 will be very different to life as it is today.

b) Read the article again and answer the questions 1 to 10.

1 Will life in the year 2200 be the same as it is today?
2 Where will children learn?
3 What will people use to visit other planets? Why?
4 Where will people live?
5 Why won't there be much pollution?
6 Why will people be healthier?
7 Why will people have more free time?
8 What is the writer's opinion about life in the year 2200?
9 In which paragraphs does the writer express his opinion?
10 How does the last paragraph start?

c) Read the text again and make notes in the table below. Then, use your notes to talk about the writer's predictions for the year 2200.

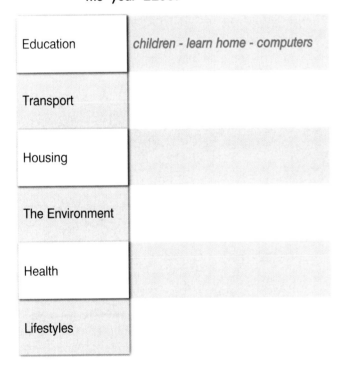

Education	*children - learn home - computers*
Transport	
Housing	
The Environment	
Health	
Lifestyles	

e.g. Children will learn at home with computers.

STUDY TIP

We use the **future simple** to make **predictions** about the future.

Affirmative	Negative	Interrogative
I/You, etc **will play**	I/you, etc **will not (won't) play**	**Will** I/you, etc **play**?

SHORT ANSWERS	
Yes, I/you, etc **will**.	No, I/you, etc **won't**.

---

5 **a) Read the text below and put the verbs in brackets into the future simple.**

In the year 2200, we **1)** .... (not / drive) cars that use petrol. We **2)** .... (drive) electric cars. We **3)** .... (not / use) aeroplanes to travel long distances. We **4)** .... (travel) in space shuttles instead. There **5)** .... (not / be) any motorbikes in the year 2200, but bicycles **6)** .... (become) very popular again.

The most popular holiday destination in the year 2200 **7)** .... (be) the moon. I believe that people **8)** .... (also / visit) other countries, just as they do today.

b) Read the text again and put a tick (✓) next to what will happen or a cross (✗) next to what won't happen in the year 2200. Use the notes to talk about transport and travel in the year 2200.

transport/travel	2200
cars that use petrol	✗
electric cars	✓
aeroplanes	
space shuttles	
motorbikes	
bicycles	
the moon	
other countries	

e.g. People won't drive cars that use petrol.
People will drive electric cars.

---

6 Read the following predictions about life in the year 2200 and mark them as **O** (optimistic) or **P** (pessimistic).

1 ☐ People will ride bicycles, so there will be less air pollution.

2 ☐ Space travel will be cheap, so people will go on holiday to the moon.

3 ☐ There will be too many people on Earth, so there won't be enough fresh water for everyone.

4 ☐ Pollution will be much worse, so people will live in underwater cities.

5 ☐ There will be new medicines, so there will be cures for diseases such as cancer and AIDS.

6 ☐ There won't be any fruit or vegetables, so people will take food pills.

7 ☐ Robots will do most jobs, so there will be fewer jobs for people.

7 Match the prompts in column **A** to those in column **B**, then make sentences using *because*, as in the example.

A	B
1 students / not use / book libraries	**a** there / not be / enough space on Earth
2 people / not swim / in the sea	**b** there / be / CD libraries
3 people / live under-ground	**c** there / not be / enough food for them
4 some animals / disappear	**d** there / be / fewer jobs
5 people / be poorer	**e** the sea / be / polluted

*e.g. Students won't use book libraries **because** there will be CD libraries.*

8 a) Match the causes (1-6) to the effects (a-f), then make sentences using so, as in the example.

b) Which of these people are optimistic about life in the future? Which are pessimistic?

CAUSES

1 e	Cities will become crowded.
2 ☐	The sea will be polluted.
3 ☐	Robots will work as cleaners and builders.
4 ☐	There will be more cars.
5 ☐	People will work twenty hours a week.
6 ☐	There won't be enough trees.

EFFECTS

a There won't be any fish.

b There won't be enough oxygen.

c Pollution will get worse.

d People will have less boring jobs.

e People will live underground.

f People will enjoy more free time.

*e.g. Cities will become overcrowded, **so** people will live underground.*

9 Match the sentences in column **A** to those in column **B**, then make sentences using so or because, as in the example.

A	B
Education	
1 Children will learn at home with computers.	a They won't go to school.
2 Children won't make any friends.	b There won't be any classes.
Transport	
1 There will be more cars than people.	a Traffic problems will be worse.
2 There will be more traffic accidents.	b Cars will be able to travel faster.
Housing	
1 There won't be enough space on Earth.	a The air on Earth will be polluted.
2 People will live on other planets.	b People will build underwater cities.
The Environment	
1 There won't be any fish.	a People will wear oxygen masks.
2 The air will be very polluted.	b The seas and rivers will be polluted.
Health	
1 There won't be enough food.	a There will be more diseases.
2 People will die younger.	b People will die of hunger.
Lifestyles	
1 People who have jobs will work longer hours.	a They will have less free time.
2 Many people won't be able to find a job.	b Companies will use robots instead of people.

e.g. *Children will learn at home with computers, so there won't be any classes.*

....

....

....

....

WRITING

TIP

When we write an **article** expressing **our opinion about changes in the future**, we can divide it into three paragraphs.

- In the **first** paragraph we say **what our opinion is**.
- In the **second** paragraph we write our **predictions**. We talk about **education, transport, housing, the environment, health** and **lifestyles**. We can also mention **reasons** and **effects** to justify our views.
- In the **third** paragraph we say **what our opinion is**, using different words from those we used in the first paragraph. We start this paragraph with *In conclusion*. We use the **future simple** to make our predictions. We can list our predictions with: **also, what is more, finally**. We express our opinion with: **I think, I believe, In my opinion**.

10 Use one point of view from each section in Ex. 9, the beginning and ending given and the paragraph plan to complete the article with the title:
"Life Will Be Worse in the Year 2200"
(**100 - 120 words**).
Use the article in Ex. 4 as a model.

Plan

Life Will Be Worse in the Year 2200

Paragraph 1: *There will be a lot of changes on our planet in the next two hundred years. I believe that these changes will make it a horrible place to live.*

Paragraph 2: predictions with reasons and effects (talk about education, transport, housing, the environment, health and lifestyles)

Paragraph 3: *In conclusion, I believe that life will be worse in the year 2200. Hopefully, though, people will be sensible and these predictions will never come true.*

Irregular Verbs

Infinitive	Past	Past Participle	Infinitive	Past	Past Participle
be	was/were	been	leave	left	left
bear	bore	born(e)	lend	lent	lent
beat	beat	beaten	let	let	let
become	became	become	lie	lay	lain
begin	began	begun	light	lit	lit
bite	bit	bitten	lose	lost	lost
blow	blew	blown	make	made	made
break	broke	broken	mean	meant	meant
bring	brought	brought	meet	met	met
build	built	built	panic	panicked	panicked
burn	burnt	burnt	pay	paid	paid
burst	burst	burst	put	put	put
buy	bought	bought	read	read	read
can	could	(been able to)	ride	rode	ridden
catch	caught	caught	ring	rang	rung
choose	chose	chosen	rise	rose	risen
come	came	come	run	ran	run
cost	cost	cost	say	said	said
cut	cut	cut	see	saw	seen
deal	dealt	dealt	sell	sold	sold
dig	dug	dug	send	sent	sent
do	did	done	set	set	set
draw	drew	drawn	sew	sewed	sewn
dream	dreamt (dreamed)	dreamt (dreamed)	shake	shook	shaken
drink	drank	drunk	shine	shone	shone
drive	drove	driven	shoot	shot	shot
eat	ate	eaten	show	showed	shown
fall	fell	fallen	shut	shut	shut
feed	fed	fed	sing	sang	sung
feel	felt	felt	sit	sat	sat
fight	fought	fought	sleep	slept	slept
find	found	found	smell	smelt (smelled)	smelt (smelled)
fly	flew	flown	speak	spoke	spoken
forbid	forbade	forbidden	speed	sped	sped
forget	forgot	forgotten	spend	spent	spent
forgive	forgave	forgiven	spill	spilt	spilt
freeze	froze	frozen	spoil	spoilt (spoiled)	spoilt (spoiled)
get	got	got	spread	spread	spread
give	gave	given	stand	stood	stood
go	went	gone	steal	stole	stolen
grow	grew	grown	stick	stuck	stuck
hang	hung	hung	strike	struck	struck
have	had	had	swear	swore	sworn
hear	heard	heard	sweep	swept	swept
hide	hid	hidden	swim	swam	swum
hit	hit	hit	take	took	taken
hold	held	held	teach	taught	taught
hurt	hurt	hurt	tear	tore	torn
keep	kept	kept	tell	told	told
know	knew	known	think	thought	thought
lay	laid	laid	throw	threw	thrown
lead	led	led	understand	understood	understood
learn	learnt (learned)	learnt (learned)	wake	woke	woken
			wear	wore	worn
			win	won	won
			write	wrote	written

PHOTO FILE SECTION

**(The pictures in this section are to be
cut out and used for your writing projects in
Units 2, 3, 6, 7, 9, 10 and 12.)**

Nicolas Cage

MEGA SPORTS CENTRE

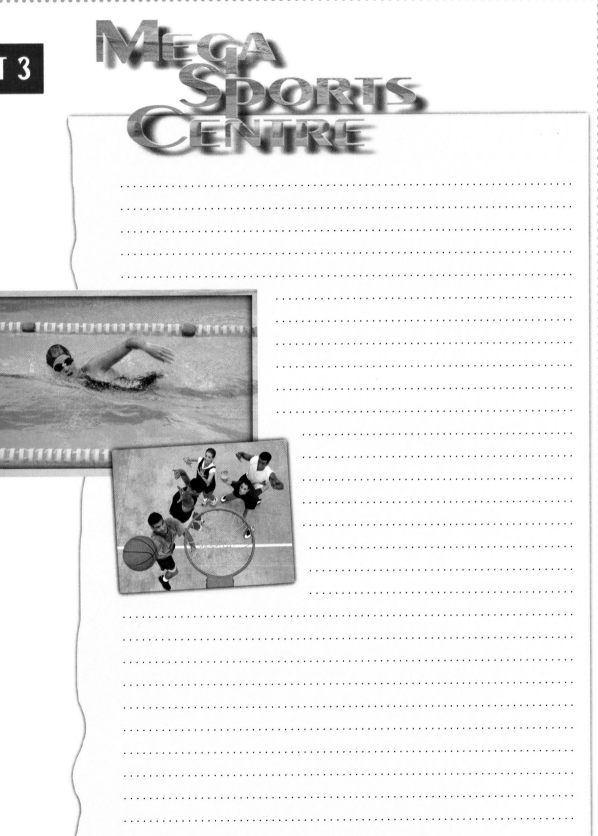

....
....
....
....
....
....
....
....
....
....
....
....
....
....
....
....
....
....
....
....
....
....
....
....
....
....
....
....

Mediterranean Omelette

Ingredients

- 2..
- 1..
- 1..
- 1..
- 25gr ....
- ....and.....................................
  ....

Instructions

- ....
  ....
- ....
  ....
- ....
  ....
- ....
  ....
- ....
  ....
- ....
  ....
- ....
  ....
- ....
  ....
- ....
  ....
- ....
  ....
- ....
  ....

A Day In The Life of
Patty Stevens

Cats Can Make the Best Pets

There is no question that a pet can give you pleasure and amusement. There are millions of happy owners around the world today who believe that cats make the best pets.

In conclusion, I believe that despite these disadvantages, cats still make the best pets. Why don't you get a cat and find out for yourself?

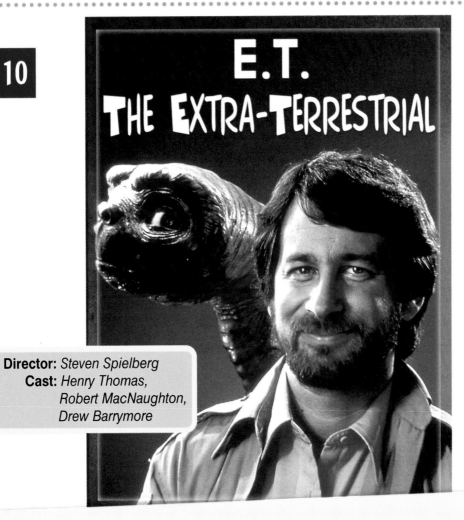

E.T.
THE EXTRA-TERRESTRIAL

Director: *Steven Spielberg*
Cast: *Henry Thomas,*
Robert MacNaughton,
Drew Barrymore

UNIT 12

Josh Bell worked as a lifeguard on a very popular beach. On his first day there, he felt a little anxious. It was a hot and sunny day and there were a lot of people in the water.

....
....
....
....
....
....
....
....
....
....
....
....
....
....
....
....
....
....
....
....
....
....
....
....
....
....
....
....
....
....